TRANSLATE
MOTIVATE
ACTIVATE

TRANSLATE
MOTIVATE
ACTIVATE

A LEADER'S GUIDE TO MOBILIZING CHANGE

LARRY SOLOMON

BROWN BOOKS
PUBLISHING GROUP

Translate, Motivate, Activate
A Leader's Guide to Mobilizing Change

Brown Books Publishing Group
16250 Knoll Trail Drive, Suite 205
Dallas, Texas 75248
www.BrownBooks.com
(972) 381-0009

A New Era in Publishing®

ISBN 978-1-61254-895-1
LCCN 2016930876

Printed in the United States
10 9 8 7 6 5 4 3 2 1

For more information or to contact the author, please go to www.SolomonPS.com.

This book is dedicated to leaders in all fields of endeavor who wish to create sustainable competitive advantage through their people. If you believe in the untapped potential of people and are looking for practical ways to help your team access their full potential, this book is for you.

If the experiences I share in this book contribute in some small way to your future success, the value of my life journey will be enhanced.

I dedicate all proceeds from the sale of this book to "My Possibilities," a for-cause organization that courageously and relentlessly pursues the full, untapped possibilities of adults with special needs. (Visit MyPossibilities.org.)

TABLE OF CONTENTS

Foreword

by

Larry Young

President and CEO – Dr Pepper Snapple Group

Over the last forty years in the beverage industry, I have consistently embraced a fundamental approach to my leadership: I run organizations with human resources (HR) on my left and finance on my right.

Within business circles, people understand the critical partnership between the CEO and the finance leader but are amazed with my core belief in the elevated strategic importance of the HR partnership. No strategy, regardless of the plan's brilliance, will ever create a sustainable competitive advantage unless people at every level of the organization—particularly those making, selling, and distributing our products and services, as well as those interfacing daily with our customers—execute that strategy with excellence.

The most significant HR value appears at my left hand as my "translator"—an HR partner skilled at translating my vision for the organization into the hearts, heads, and hands of everyone on my team. Equally important, my translator ably interprets for the rest of the executive team what works and does not work from the perspective of our frontline people. The translator's credibility connects with every level in the organization.

In 2006, we embarked upon a strategy that others in the industry had not yet succeeded at achieving: combining and merging bottling and franchise operations to create the first major fully integrated beverage business in the United States. From experience, I knew that the greatest challenges would lie in changing entrenched behaviors, aligning the team behind the right priorities, and embedding the skills critical for success.

My translator, Larry Solomon, played a major role. He took these challenges head-on. With his creativity, energy, and significant experience, Larry effectively engaged our twenty thousand employees and helped us manage wave upon wave of fundamental change. The innovative methods he developed and implemented helped align the team behind the right priorities, as well as efficiently and effectively build skill sets critical to our success.

Defying the odds and the skepticism of some analysts, we took the company public in May 2008. With the collapse of the debt market in the US, this was the worst time possible to debut on the market. When others were struggling to survive, we rallied our team to thrive. We invested in marketing, our supply chain, technology, and, most importantly, in our people and their capabilities. We increased our market cap 50 percent with no mergers and acquisitions, and our market share consistently outperformed the industry for five years. My translator contributed significantly toward this success.

In this book, Larry lays out a logical and practical approach to the effective translation of strategy into the day-to-day actions of employees at every level of an organization.

Visionary leaders need great translators. I encourage every CEO to read this book and share these proven effective methods with the leader of your HR department. Turn your HR partners into translators and thrive as we have.

Preface

believe that the true catalyst for successful strategy execution in today's dynamic world is the ability to constantly and effectively mobilize people behind change. It is only when we create this momentum that we can achieve what Larry Young refers to as a *sustainable competitive advantage*. "If you always do what you've always done," notes life coach Tony Robbins, "you'll always get what you've always got." Change is the only constant. The key to successful mobilization, then, lies in the ability to demystify strategies and translate them meaningfully into the daily activities of every employee.

As translator, I have had the privilege of assisting leaders in businesses around the world align the focus, activities, and behaviors of their employees, as well as shape their visions into strategies. Equally, I translated employee concerns, hopes, and fears regarding the proposed strategy back to their respective leaders. I believe that this two-way translation is the key to strategy execution and that it is the most important role that the human resource leader can play in an organization.

"Total People Costs" represents a major, if not the largest, expense line on the profit and loss statement of most businesses. This investment in people can also become a company's greatest asset. If you are *directing* human resources, by definition you accept accountability to maximize the return on this substantial investment. Leadership in action is being able to mobilize teams through the effective translation of strategy, and, when effectively facilitated by HR leaders, it earns them the right to be at the executive table.

Too often, HR's focus is primarily on transactional services that, while important, have little to offer to business strategy. Core to true mobilization is the fundamental belief in the abilities of individuals and teams who, given the right conditions, can and will deliver abundantly. In my experience, employing methods to tap into this potential has paid handsome dividends. But there are challenges.

This book is about handling those challenges and preparing employees to actively participate in their company's growth. Divided into four sections, each will focus on one of what I see as the four primary challenges of mobilization: engaging, aligning, enabling, and sustaining. Discussions will include learning experiences and useful processes to help you:

- Develop a holistic and comprehensive change implementation plan.
- Lead the effective management of change.
- Build employee ownership of change by creating a unified team.

I've also included a series of challenging questions at the end of each chapter that will help you evaluate and ideally strengthen your proposed strategies.

You will see throughout the book that I have shared my own experiences and perceptions in order to illustrate key principles. Of particular relevance are the examples from the formation and development of the Dr Pepper Snapple Group over an eight-year period. These were the early, formative years of a company forged by multiple acquisitions and then set on a path to independence. During that time, the mobilization initiatives were grouped under one multi-year campaign: Call to ACTION. By branding the campaign, we were able to link the numerous initiatives that drove the successful execution of our business plan. In the following chapters, I will frequently be referring to these Call to ACTION initiatives and their uses in employee mobilization.

For those of you who may not have human resource support to help with the translation of your change agendas, you will find that *Translate, Motivate, Activate* is written as a practical guide for all team leaders within an organization.

If you are an HR professional, you play an invaluable role in the translation process. It is important to ensure, however, that the ownership of the change agenda must remain, and be seen to remain, with the leader of the team. As the leader of your team, you must own, drive, and model the desired change. If the driver of change is seen as an HR endeavor, the likelihood of *sustained* change is questionable.

It is my hope that by reading this book you will better lead your teams—in any function or level within your organization—to deliver continuous high performance that without your leadership might not have been attained.

Larry Solomon

Acknowledgments

First and foremost, I thank God for the incredible opportunities He has afforded me in my career. There is no greater source of learning than the "university of life."

As with all learning, it is not without sacrifice. I thank my wife, Charmaine, and our children Tascha, Tyron, Donovan, and Kyle for their love, encouragement, and support, and for enduring the upheaval associated with international moves.

We are all products of our environments, and I am proud that two incredible role models, my parents, Denis and Norma Solomon, have influenced my life, career, and, thus, this book. My mother's life has formed the family foundation of Christian values and a love and care for others. My father's incredible work ethic, courage, and determination have entirely redirected the course for our family history, creating opportunities for his children that he was never afforded. They leave a legacy for generations to come.

My journey has afforded me multicultural opportunities to learn from diverse leaders, and I am thankful for their guidance, coaching, and support. Two of those leaders, Patrick Fleming and Larry Young, have had significant impact on my career and my life.

I thank Patrick, with whom I worked in both South Africa and in England, for demonstrating to me and to all around him the true meaning of business ethics through his honest, caring, and trustworthy approach in the handling of even the toughest of business situations.

I thank Larry, with whom I worked in the United States, who, with his fundamental belief in people, inspires others to achieve greatly. Having graduated from the school of hard knocks, his courage in the face of adversity and his ability to connect with people at all levels of the organization is truly inspiring.

As leaders, our success is enabled by the caliber of people around us. From South Africa to England to America, I have been surrounded by teams of outstanding people from whom I learned so much in my growth as a leader.

And finally, I want to acknowledge two artists, my son Tyron Solomon and David Rodriguez, for their help with illustrations in this book, and Doreen Piellucci, whose creative and disciplined editing helped me get this book across the finish line.

Introduction

What Is Mobilization?

Throughout my career, I have been amazed by the positive organizational changes that individuals and teams had achieved when they performed in environments that lived and breathed encouragement, challenge, recognition, and support. Conversely, I have seen the collapse of outstanding opportunities when leaders failed to unite teams behind their ideas.

While many leaders hold professional degrees, business programs arguably focus on what one would call the "hard skills"—the execution of strategy through finance, marketing, logistics, etc. The "soft skills"—those that execute strategy through *people*—are given far too little attention. The reality is that these are the difficult skills that we so often struggle with. After all, we're dealing with the complexity of human creativity, opinions, perspectives, biases, and aspirations, to name only a few attributes that complicate our ability to mobilize a team behind one agenda.

Think for a moment about the inherent conflict that exists in the very DNA of business design—conflict that, if not effectively channeled, leads to counterproductive behaviors that stifle creativity and embed inertia. Consider the conflicting views within sales and marketing regarding short-term trade development spend and long-term brand building spend, or the desire of production to maximize asset utilization by minimizing product diversification, while research and development argue for more innovation and variety to attract customers, and on it goes. These siloed approaches are not in themselves wrong, as functions must continually pursue avenues to maximize their business impact. What's so often missing, however, is the ability of leadership to effectively translate business priorities in a manner that mobilizes and unites a team behind a holistic strategy. If channeled through effective mobilization, this inherent conflict can instead become a core strength, and the potentially destructive conflict will transform into what I call *constructive* contention.

Turning contention into a constructive force requires an environment in which all ideas, particularly those that are contrary to the norm, are welcomed and explored. This environment is further enabled when everyone's initial reaction to an alternative is governed by the assumption that the challenge is in pursuit of the best possible business solution. If everyone involved in a potentially contentious discussion begins by assuming *positive* intent, the outcome can be a healthier dialogue and a more thorough diagnosis of alternatives.

Surprisingly, leaders often allow, and even fuel, unhealthy conflict by:

- Believing that people understand the interdependencies between functions.
- Fostering destructive survival of the fittest behaviors, taking for granted that the best solutions will surface. This falsely presupposes a correlation between forcefulness of character and quality of contribution.
- Hoping that by ignoring them, conflicts will resolve themselves over time.

These assumptions, unfortunately, often result in highly politicized work environments in which the most forceful individuals drive their own viewpoints and agendas, generating mediocre performance at best. This is a far cry from a mobilized team.

It is from these experiences that I have built a simple, pragmatic framework that captures the core elements of mobilization.

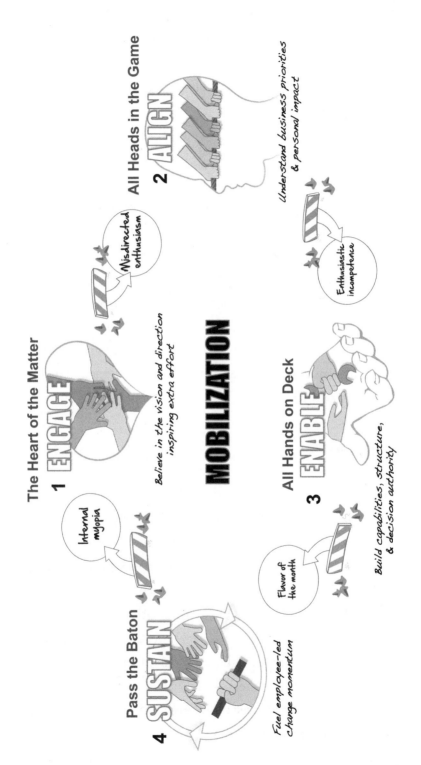

THE MOBILIZATION FRAMEWORK

For context, the following is a brief description of each challenge in The Mobilization Framework:

Challenge 1—Engage [The Heart of the Matter]

To create a belief in the vision and direction of the organization that inspires extra effort, enthusiasm, and commitment.

Leaders must focus strongly on employee engagement, recognizing it as a critical ingredient to the effective launch of their initiative. True mobilization depends on it. However, creating a belief in the vision and direction of the organization, department, or function can be fleeting. If we do no more than engage employees, this enthusiasm can often be misdirected, so engagement must be complemented with alignment.

Challenge 2—Align [All Heads in the Game]

To help employees understand business priorities and how they can contribute both personally and collectively to them.

A failure to effectively align the efforts of a team results in enthusiastic incompetence. We must build crystal-clear alignment in order to channel the energies of all employees for maximum business impact and to avoid the dissipation of energies against less value-adding ventures. If properly executed, this process filters, demystifies, and translates the handful of critical priorities that offer the business the highest value. It is the effective execution of these priorities at every layer of the organization that offers the best opportunity for success.

Challenge 3—Enable [All Hands on Deck]

To efficiently and effectively equip employees at all levels with the specific knowledge, skills, and processes necessary to deliver against business priorities.

We must enable our employees to perform by providing them with pragmatic, easily accessible tools, processes, and techniques, as well as make certain that the organizational structure enables rather than restricts decision making at the appropriate levels. We must also create appropriate and meaningful consequences associated with expected behaviors and outcomes.

Challenge 4—Sustain [Pass the Baton]

To ensure the continuity of change beyond the oversight of the leader, transferring leadership and ownership of change to the team.

We must avoid the unfortunate fate that so many change initiatives encounter—having gained initial traction, without continual oversight, they lose both momentum and their perceived importance. The challenge is to keep change alive and relevant in the competitive landscape. To truly sustain the new practices and behaviors implemented, we must build the team's capabilities to lead and continue to drive change without continual oversight.

Mobilization is, therefore, the multiplying effect of all of the above challenges. Through deliberate and sustained focus at every level within the organization, we build:

- Exceptionally high degrees of **engagement** (true commitment to the journey—hearts).

- Crystal-clear **alignment** (understanding of what to do—heads).
- Pragmatic **enablement** (confidence in how to do it—hands).
- Sustaining **momentum** (passing on the leadership of change).

True mobilization is never the product of evolution, which by definition is the outcome of the survival of the fittest. An evolutionary approach to mobilization is a drawn-out, destructive change process in which value is lost, inertia prevails, and myopic perspectives flourish. True mobilization is always a product of intelligent design.

To illustrate the power of true mobilization, let me share with you the story of an exceptional sales merchandiser working in a retail grocery store. I call this "The Phineas Effect."

As a merchandiser, Phineas knew his job well—how to stock shelves, merchandise effectively, accurately price all items, etc.—but he also understood the importance of customer service.

One day, when he was stocking shelves, Phineas noticed a customer who seemed frustrated. He asked if he could help. The woman said she couldn't find Rose's Lime Cordial. Phineas looked but couldn't find it either. He told the customer to continue shopping and he'd bring the item from the back of the store.

But the item was not in the storeroom. What Phineas did next was the result of an employee who was committed to the success of his company. He ran from the store's rear exit to another retail store, located and paid for two bottles of Rose's Lime Cordial, and returned in time to find the woman at the checkout counter.

Though she intended to pay for the items, Phineas gave her the receipt and said they were a gift from his company "because we should have had them on the shelves."

The customer was so impressed that she contacted senior management. Senior management was impressed as well: Phineas's story was communicated to all employees within the organization. As a result, instances of the "Phineas Effect" multiplied, and the company became recognized for its commitment to excellent customer service.

Can you imagine the competitive advantage if all your employees thought and acted like Phineas?

Let's refer back to "The Mobilization Framework." Clearly, the success of this model is evident in Phineas's actions:

- Phineas went beyond his job description in pursuit of the company's vision (**engaged**).
- He understood that he could contribute to the vision in the course of his daily activities (**aligned**).
- Phineas had the decision authority to act quickly and effectively to meet the customer's needs (**enabled**).
- With the company's recognition, Phineas's behavior was reinforced, and others followed his example of practical acts of superior customer service (**sustained**).

Join me, then, as we explore these four dimensions of mobilization. With effective execution, they will lead your team to superior performance.

The heart of the matter

ENGAGE

Believe in the
vision and direction,
inspire extra effort

Developing an
Engagement Strategy

Many of us have read business reports indicating that the majority of change undertakings fail to deliver the expected results. The reasons for failure are seldom that the strategies were inappropriate or that the models were unrealistic. In most cases, the failed change initiatives had to do with people issues and, more specifically, their unwillingness and/or inability to shape new behaviors to drive the necessary change.

Based on the 2014 Global Workforce Study conducted by Towers Watson, only 40 percent of employees are highly engaged. Furthermore, 24 percent are disengaged and another 36 percent can be described as either unsupportive or detached. That's a full 60 percent of employees lacking the elements required to be fully engaged in the vision and direction of the organization.

While this research is disturbing, it also identifies an excellent opportunity. It suggests that with concerted effort, it is feasible to create real advantage by raising your organization's level of engagement from average to superior—significantly higher than the average of those companies within your competitive base. To achieve and sustain this higher stage of engagement requires of you a sequence of well-orchestrated and continuous activities. It is the role of the leader to drive these activities as well as to determine the effectiveness of implementation by eliciting feedback from employees at all levels in the organization. Candid feedback is essential, as it helps you address ambiguities that take root as a consequence of differing interpretations of messages delivered.

While many companies make meaningful progress with employee engagement—continually measuring progress and holding managers accountable for survey results—there is significant danger in assuming that high levels of engagement will cause people's energies to logically or instinctively align with the right priorities to achieve your agenda. When priorities are misinterpreted, even well-intentioned employees may incorrectly direct their energies toward nonessential activities. At its worst, this pursuit of alternative goals and strategies becomes counterproductive and undermines the endgame you are trying to achieve.

Too often, leaders assume that a message has been heard, understood, and embraced after only a few one-way presentations with PowerPoint slides. Effective engagement demands consistency of message, frequent repetition, verification of receipt, and validation of interpretation.

The Engagement Cycle

Learning from my myriad attempts at engaging the hearts of teams, I have developed a cycle of activities that, if implemented with discipline and rigor, will help you better engage your people in your change journey.

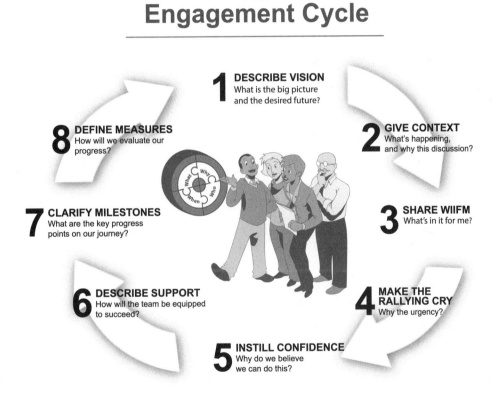

The
Engagement Cycle

1 DESCRIBE VISION
What is the big picture and the desired future?

2 GIVE CONTEXT
What's happening, and why this discussion?

3 SHARE WIIFM
What's in it for me?

4 MAKE THE RALLYING CRY
Why the urgency?

5 INSTILL CONFIDENCE
Why do we believe we can do this?

6 DESCRIBE SUPPORT
How will the team be equipped to succeed?

7 CLARIFY MILESTONES
What are the key progress points on our journey?

8 DEFINE MEASURES
How will we evaluate our progress?

Step 1. Engaging begins with vision—a clear and compelling picture of the desired future.

In "Any Road," George Harrison sings, "If you don't know where you are going, any road will get you there." Where you end up may well be the outcome of an evolutionary process rather than intelligent design, as you and your team react to circumstances and pressures when changes develop.

People generally want to be part of something greater than themselves. Engagement, then, begins with the design and communication of an idea that is both inspiring and challenging. Whether expressing a vision for a team, a division, a corporation, or an entire industry, the picture of the change must be:

- Presented clearly.
- Delivered with consistency over time.
- Responsive to employee feedback.
- Effectively translated when adaptations of the plan must be implemented.
- Inspiring and challenging.

As a leader, your vision should not only be aspirational but should also serve as a beacon that will steer employee behaviors and focus their efforts.

Former Harvard Business School Professor Dr. John Kotter further suggests that you identify a "guiding coalition"—leaders, both formal and informal, within your organization that will support, lead, and reinforce your vision. They must be engaged in the undertaking, sometimes through one-on-one discussions and coaching. Failing to do so leaves your change agenda vulnerable to powerful undercurrents of resistance as employees rally behind the contradictory views of these influential people.

We live in a world that is dynamic, and changing market circumstances may require adjustments to the vision. Though consistency of message is always preferred, necessary changes should not be ignored. Communicate what changes will take place, and effectively translate the impact of any adaptations to the plan. Encourage your employees with a clear vision of a future you plan to create together.

The title "leader" implies that there are others following you somewhere—ideally not because of your title, but because of your ability to envision a future state and a quest that engages their interests, energies, and passion. The litmus test of one's leadership is to look over one's shoulder to see if anyone is following you!

Further, if you have the support of an HR partner as your translator, seek out his or her candid feedback as well, to determine if your communication of the vision has resonated with your audience.

Step 2. Providing context, context, context!

Once you have effectively engaged their hearts, the greater challenge will be in keeping your team engaged. To ensure that a clear vision resonates with a team, we must provide meaningful context that connects with the entire audience. Clarifying the *why* and *why now* behind your vision and its consequential changes avoids confusion regarding your motives. When you explain context up front, you significantly reduce the probability of people arriving at erroneous conclusions. In the absence of clear context, employees may tend to gravitate toward the negative, leaving the internal grapevine to spread, magnify, and dramatize this negativity. Left to fester, these perceptions can become the lens through which all future communications on the change agenda are filtered.

When leaders present a well-designed implementation plan to a group of employees, they sometimes assume that the background and circumstances that led to this plan are either obvious or irrelevant for the audience. As a consequence, they fail to build an understanding of what has triggered the need for change, why it is important, and how it will be integrated with other key activities. The outcome results in varying degrees of engagement, as individuals interpret what might have driven this change and why they are now being asked to rally behind it. Failure to link the proposed change with the current business agenda often leads to a skeptical response from team members who anticipate that a new set of priorities will follow shortly.

A colleague of mine related the following story that illustrates how essential context can be.

At a company-wide meeting, the CEO of the company was reviewing business performance for the first quarter. The results were not good, and he was very clear about the need for everyone to raise their level of productivity.

He then went on to introduce a program called "teaming" that would identify individuals who needed exposure to different disciplines within the company and pair them with employees who could share their knowledge and experiences.

The CEO had presented two separate topics. But because the teaming endeavor lacked context, many employees mistakenly believed that the two were linked. As a result, there was much confusion and alarm when they assumed that teaming was a negative consequence for poor performance and a plan to reduce head count by making individuals redundant.

Later, my colleague met with the CEO, gleaned the motives behind the idea, and crafted a meaningful communication to the employees. Unfortunately, with the failure to provide context at its launch, this undertaking ultimately failed.

An essential step, therefore, in engaging the hearts of the team is to provide context, clearly explaining:

- Why this change.
- Why now.
- How it fits in with all the other projects they have going on.

Step 3. Addressing the all-important "What's in it for me?"

In planning our communication, we consider what, why, who, how, and when, yet often neglect the "What's In It For Me?" (WIIFM) factor. Think back to situations when you addressed a group of employees about an important change being introduced. Did you notice how their expressions morphed from interest to angst after the first mention of change? If you observed closely, you would have noticed glazed expressions as their thoughts shifted and appeared to ask, "What's in this for me?" At the moment when their attention shifted to the personal implications of your proposed change, you would have lost your audience. As they began jumping to their own "confusions," anything you said beyond that point might just as well have been "rhubarb, rhubarb, rhubarb."

To avoid this reaction, then, you must transparently and honestly address the WIIFM factor, letting employees know as early as possible not only future implications of the change but also how they will benefit from the initiative. This step will significantly enhance your ability to engage your team and retain their attention in this process.

Change—positive, negative, or a combination of both—can be disruptive, but you'll strengthen engagement if you anticipate and communicate a well-constructed plan that will guide and support the team through these implications.

Step 4. Conveying urgency; making the rallying cry.

Whether the need for significant change is driven by chance to outperform competitors, seize a new opportunity, or survive in a changing market, how you call your team to action must be convincing, unambiguous, and engaging. It is essential to always put yourself squarely in the shoes of the listeners. What will inspire them to act? For this to happen, you must understand your audiences and adapt your delivery accordingly. Business jargon will likely distance you from the hearts and minds of your listeners, so it is important to speak plainly in terms that everyone can understand.

It is the leader's role to identify, translate, and distill employees' thoughts and concerns about the pending change agenda and use these insights in the crafting of key messages. In some cases, the spirit of the message is a rallying cry, calling the team to new heights of performance, building upon current strong delivery; sometimes, the message has a greater sense of urgency—the critical need to turn performance around in order to avoid the adverse consequences of current standards of performance.

Whether it is a product, service, or idea, motivating others requires effective selling on your part. No professional salesperson would present to a key customer without thoroughly preparing and thinking through all dimensions of the selling proposal—this is especially important when a new launch will impact the lives of your employees. An inspiring call to action will strengthen their belief in your ability to lead them through this change.

Resistance may surface due to the disruptive nature of change, and this is often fueled by a fear of the unknown. Change demands the letting go of well-established practices and moving beyond the comfort of the known into the discomfort of the unknown. The need to acquire new skills, demonstrate new behaviors, and embrace new ways of working can be seen as overwhelming.

Step 5. Instilling confidence—building a "we can do this" attitude.

As you reflect on the magnitude of your change agenda, consider carefully the new requirements and the implications of this change on your people. How do you, as their leader, instill in them a belief and a confidence in the team's ability to achieve the stretching goals and significant change called for? Great leadership requires an ability to inspire others to achieve levels of performance they would otherwise not have achieved.

Encourage your team with genuine words of confidence. Arouse confidence within your group by reflecting on past achievements. Consider carefully the changes and stretching goals that the team has successfully achieved in the past:

- What were the highlights of those endeavors?
- What lessons can be brought to bear on the new challenges?
- What core attributes of the team enabled those past successes?
- Which of those core attributes will lead to considerable success with the new agenda?

Insert these experiences into your communications. A well-thought-out review of your past successes and what you learned fuels the team's belief in its collective abilities. Depending on the clarity, consistency, and enthusiasm in your messages, this belief will either ignite or extinguish your team's enthusiasm.

Step 6. Ensuring support—you will not be dropped into the deep end.

Being confident that the team can achieve success together does little to address the underlying concerns of the individual who may be wondering:

- Am I going to be a part of that winning team?
- Will my past experiences and skills count going forward?
- What new processes and procedures will I be expected to perform?

No leader can guarantee that everyone on the team will be able to, or choose to, make the necessary changes. However, individuals need to be given an opportunity to perform, and leaders must clearly describe and adequately fund the support necessary to equip them to succeed.

The greater the magnitude of change, the greater the investment in this needed support.

I have found that as pressures inevitably mount to reduce the costs of significant change campaigns, investments in training become soft targets for cost reduction, leading to inadequate skills and knowledge development. This is especially true with change projects that, while essential to the business, have no easily measurable return on investment. Core infrastructural system upgrades often fall prey to this business pressure.

Failing to invest sufficiently in training for critical business systems and processes is comparable to training a 747 pilot on the job by trial and error. A deliberate, well-thought-out and appropriately funded training and coaching schedule needs to be budgeted for and built into your change agenda. Your clear and convincing commitment to the support necessary in order for your team to be successful must be an integral part of your engagement communication.

Step 7. Clarifying milestones—breaking the task into digestible chunks.

As stated earlier, the magnitude of change often overwhelms employees. They may not ask, but will need to know, more about the venture and how it will impact their lives. This is "the elephant in the room." Tackle it head-on by communicating your agenda and progress as the plan develops, and acknowledge each milestone of success. By doing this, you:

- Communicate the extent of planning that went into this change initiative.
- Make the achievement of the end goal more feasible by providing progress points that are within reach.
- Maintain engagement for the duration of the change by keeping people on track.
- Create opportunities to celebrate early wins, making heroes of those who drive change.
- Help redirect efforts and focus when necessary without creating concern about the entire change program.

- Provide new information that keeps communication updates informative and engaging.

Step 8. Performance measures—in sight, top of mind.

The final step in The Engagement Cycle is to describe what success looks like and how progress toward these goals will be measured and monitored.

A visual display that illustrates the ultimate goal as well as performance against milestones helps to maintain team focus and keep the change agenda top of mind. These displays should include both lead and lag indicators. Lead indicators measure the effectiveness of tactics toward an end goal and help identify opportunities for timely corrective action. Lag indicators measure key milestones and are important for the recognition of success, as well as for determining whether the lead indicators are measuring the right tactics.

When members of a team are held accountable for the design, maintenance, and communication of these visual displays of progress, the degree of their involvement and commitment to successful outcomes will increase substantially.

Visual performance displays will also keep you vigilant. As a leader, you must encourage regular use and maintenance of visual performance displays. This is a powerful tool that will keep your project in the forefront and well understood.

This eight-step cycle needs to be repeated throughout the entire period, from the launch of your change initiative to embedding. When you believe you have communicated to the point of redundancy, your communication journey will have just begun.

Practical Application
Developing an Engagement Strategy

Use these questions in the development of your "Engagement Cycle."

1. What different audiences do you need to engage, and what is the level of their support for your initiative?
2. Who is your guiding coalition, and how able are they to drive change deep into the organization?
3. How clear and engaging is the vision you have created? Does it describe a clear picture of the desired future state?
4. Are you creating and communicating clear context for why this change must take place?
5. Are you clearly conveying what's in it for them? Are you considering all stakeholders?
6. Is the sense of urgency for change clearly communicated and understood?
7. Are you conveying your faith, belief, and confidence in your team to succeed?
8. Are you committing to and communicating how you will equip the team with the knowledge, skills, and processes necessary to execute successfully?
9. Have you identified and communicated key milestones along the journey?
10. Have you established clear measures of progress and methods to share results with the team?

Engaging by Example

The Cues and Clues

As leaders, we often underestimate the impact of our words and actions. We are constantly sending messages to our people through what we say and do—and what we *don't* say and *don't* do. Inadvertently, we may be sending messages that erode engagement and create a counterproductive buzz at the water cooler. For our plan to be successful, then, we must lead the change by our example.

Water Cooler Talk

We must also confirm that our messages are being accurately translated. To do this, we must pay close attention to how our employees respond to the messages as well as create an environment that invites and enables our team to provide candid feedback. In this way, we can clarify any misinterpretations or ambiguities that may disrupt the plan's positive momentum.

People Take Their Cues from You

In theater, cue cards—visible only to those onstage—highlight key words of dialogue to remind and assure actors during their performance. This is analogous to the leader who sends out overt cues to the staff. Especially when change is implemented, people look to their leader for these cues. They will model their behaviors around what they see their leaders do. For this reason, we need to model the expected behaviors.

We need to demonstrate the "new" in word and deed. Approaching a change initiative with a "good for the troops" attitude is a recipe for certain failure. Too often, leaders are asked to say the right words or circulate a prewritten e-mail as a demonstration of their support. Because the team will instinctively know what is truly embraced by leadership and what carries only a passive endorsement from senior leadership, it is essential that leaders demonstrate their personal commitment to the future outcome.

Because change can be chaotic, there are bound to be "moments of truth"—disruptive moments in the journey of change where the future success of an initiative will depend on the leader's response. Typically, we can tell more about a person's motives and intentions by their unplanned reactions to circumstances than we can from their planned actions. While preparation is important, how you react when the change initiative staggers through a painful period will send loud cues to your people about the strength of your commitment to the change. We must be proactive to ensure that the right cues are being sent and received, particularly when facing headwinds.

We Also Send Clues in Covert Messages

As opposed to cues—overt messages we deliberately communicate to our teams—clues are the subtle messages we send that may shape the behaviors of others. Whether by innuendo, inference, or body language, clues are subject to all forms of interpretation. Even humor can send destructive clues. If team members joke about important changes, they may attract support that builds negativity around the project. All these subtleties can corrode the core of your planned change as employees test new ideas to determine if they will be temporary measures or more long-lasting commitments. They may wonder if leaders are merely toeing the corporate line or if they personally believe in the change they are calling for. So, start with yourself. Check your own comments, body language, and mannerisms, and do not tolerate others sending counterproductive clues using sarcasm or criticism. Take immediate corrective action. Deal with the problem before it takes root and grows into an accepted norm.

There are occasions, however, when it is necessary to act in ways that, if not explained, can generate negative clues. The following example illustrates the importance of being aware of these moments and ensuring that the interpretations of one's actions are not misleading.

Recently, while working on a change project with a client company, the head of the department explained to his team before the meeting began that he would have to step out for a few minutes to address an issue with a key customer and that this would necessitate glancing at his cell phone occasionally, as he was expecting a text message from the customer.

There are very few instances when checking e-mail messages or texts is acceptable during business meetings. Because this leader alerted the group prior to the meeting, he was both respectful and transparent and, as a result, avoided any negative clues regarding the perceived importance he attributed to the project being discussed.

Practical Application
Engaging by Example

1. Consider the deliberate cues you want to hold up for your employees to use as reference to what "great" looks like.
2. Think carefully about the inadvertent clues you could be sending.
3. Ask for feedback from those who will give you candid insights into the comments or actions you take that could be sending ambiguous or contradictory messages.
4. How can you send positive cues and clues that manage the grapevine communications and the water cooler chatter to your advantage?

Addressing Change Resistance

Chances are that though you have successfully engaged your people and have covered all dimensions of "The Engagement Cycle," you will still encounter some forms of resistance to your change agenda. Although we prefer not to admit it, most of us have change resistance built into our DNA. Here's a quick exercise to prove the point:

Fold your arms in front of you. Comfortable? Now look at your folded arms. Which arm is set on top of the other? Now reverse the order of your arms, placing the one that is currently on top to the bottom. Does that feel uncomfortable? Who taught you which arm to put on top? Likely, no one did. It is a habit you have developed over the years that feels natural and comfortable to you. Breaking even this simple habit can create discomfort. Actually, unless there is a compelling reason and meaningful consequence, you would have no reason to make this change.

A simple exercise, but perhaps it illustrates the point that we all possess a little resistance to change. Few of us love change. A wise professor once told me that we only really change when the discomfort of staying as we are is greater than the discomfort associated with the "new." Change can be uncomfortable even when we know we must embrace it—this is an unavoidable reality. So, as leaders, we must make it more uncomfortable for our people *not* to change than to endure the awkwardness of transitioning to the new expected standards.

We build this discomfort through the creation and consistent application of both positive and negative consequences associated with the change expectation. At the same time, we must coach our people through the discomfort of change as they develop their new skills, processes, or behaviors—keep them focused on the positive and prevent them from regressing to their former behaviors.

In managing change resistance, it is critically important to discover the underlying reasons for an individual's resistance to the new. Though we may view some actions as irrational, most people have reasons for their behaviors. They are acting in accordance with their interpretation of the information and messages they have received.

Resistance to Change

To address change resistance, we must determine what is giving rise to the observed behavior—the underlying mind-sets, perceptions, or circumstances. If we can identify the drivers of resistance, we can address its root causes rather than dabble with the symptoms of resistance.

We will review some of the most commonly found drivers of change resistance.

Fear of Incompetence. Even with training, some employees may oppose change because they are not confident in their capabilities. Their fear may be reflected in statements like "I hate this new computer system!" or "The old way worked just fine!"

Fear of the Unknown. Some resist change because of a concern that the proposed change may expose weaknesses or inadequacies in their performance. This fear evidences itself in procrastination or the pursuit of workarounds to avoid the perceived harsh consequences of embracing the new.

Seasoned Resistance. You may also come across resistance from your most seasoned team members. While many years in a particular role can build substantial experience, it can also embed employees with entrenched views and myopic approaches. These individuals merely indulge new methods, which they see as irrelevant, naive, or unattainable. Their approach is to offer superficial support but never drive the change deep into their areas of responsibility. In so doing, the damage that they can inflict can cripple your change agenda. They honestly believe they are doing the right thing for the company by *not* embracing what they see as unneeded change and, as seasoned employees, they are often capable of adversely eroding the commitment of others.

Questioned Relevance. Some employees recognize the need for *others* to change but exclude themselves from that obligation. These change-killers think that the new approaches being introduced will probably be good for the troops, but, with their own experience and expertise, the initiative should have little if any impact on them.

Work Overload. Others use their current busy-ness as a legitimate excuse. "We're already overloaded, and nothing is being taken off our plates" is their response to change. The result is that they will provide the least support necessary to avoid consequences, while hoping that this, like so many change endeavors, will be short lived.

When we understand the perspective from which individuals approach a proposed change, we are provided with valuable insight into their motives for resistance. We must spend time with members of the team, particularly the influential (often informal) leaders within the group. By openly discussing the change agenda and listening carefully to their responses, we are better able to diagnose the levels and types of resistance that may be encountered. This enables us to anticipate and proactively build necessary preventive, corrective, and contingency plans.

Levels of Agreement

As you listen carefully to responses regarding the change agenda, what should you listen for? How might you determine the level of commitment you are engendering? You may find the following chart to be a helpful guide in determining where more time needs to be invested in the handling of potential resistance—use it as a gauge to judge degrees of buy-in and commitment to the suggested change initiative.

As people respond to your statements and questions, listen actively to determine the extent of their commitments. Where you have doubts, probe deeper to uncover the root causes. Of particular concern is the response that falls into the category of "I don't disagree." Consider this a significant red flag. As leader, you want to be assured that when you are in the thick of change disruption, others will be at your side doing whatever is needed to make the launch a success.

While resistance will always be present with change, through effective diagnosis and proactive intervention, you can ensure that a critical mass of participants of the change fully agree and commit to its successful achievement.

Levels of Agreement

"I fully agree!"	"I will actively participate with you in achieving it"	Commit
"I agree"	"I am happy to provide you help where I can"	Support
"I'm OK"	"I can see why you want to do it"	Empathize
"I don't disagree"	"I don't care one way or the other"	Acquiesce
"I disagree"	"I don't see value in supporting this"	Distance
"I strongly disagree!"	"I will challenge this approach"	Resist

Resistance for the Cause

As mentioned earlier, the most insidious and destructive form of resistance to change surfaces when seasoned individuals protect current practices and behaviors and believe that their overt or covert opposition to change protects and serves the greater good of the organization. When individuals in senior positions or influential roles within an organization demonstrate such resistance, the destructive impact can be devastating to a change initiative. These decisions to resist change concerning the best long-term course for the brand, function, or business are fueled by an interpretation based on their years of experience. Seldom malicious, this resistance pivots on logic and a deep desire to protect time-tested approaches.

In 2000, Cadbury Schweppes acquired and integrated the Snapple brand into their United States beverage business. The initial response to this consolidation serves as a fine example of the resistance *for* the cause.

While recognizing the exceptional upside potential of the Snapple brand, the leadership team of Cadbury Schweppes was determined not to repeat the brand integration challenges faced by the Quaker Oats Company. Quaker had acquired the brand in 1997 for $1.7 billion and sold it four years later to Triarc Companies, Inc. for just $300 million.

In 2000, Triarc Companies, Inc. sold the Snapple Beverage Group to Cadbury Schweppes for an enterprise value of $1.45 billion. The US team of Cadbury Schweppes now shouldered the responsibility to integrate the Snapple business into its American beverage business, as well as to rebuild the brand to the number-one position it once held in the premium tea category.

Because members of the team feared a repeated loss of shareholder value, they became disproportionately focused on the historic reasons for Snapple's success prior to the Quaker acquisition. Unfortunately, they failed to recognize that the iced tea market, as well as the composition of its competitors, had fundamentally changed. Some members of the team resisted essential changes in product formulation, packaging, pricing, and distribution, pledging that they would not destroy the "DNA of Snapple."

The selective interpretation of this refrain—do not destroy the DNA of Snapple—created significant misalignment across the organization. Employees were engaged, all right—unfortunately, in actions that eroded any meaningful effort to drive the change so desperately needed to regain Snapple's dominant position. The ambiguity of the DNA statement caused highly talented individuals to pull in different directions, building significant inertia at a time when the market was gaining momentum.

This form of resistance can only be overcome by a deliberate intervention from the top tier of the organization. The CEO of the

US Division intervened, and a series of clear directives and decisive actions immediately followed, calling for the focused efforts of everyone involved. As a result, the team was able to execute a well-communicated strategy for the repositioning of the brand. The unhealthy internal conflict dissipated, and the company was able to once again leverage the power and equity inherent in the Snapple trademark.

So, as you think about your change agenda, what resistance *for* the cause might you encounter? Breaking this resistance to change calls for implementation of meaningful consequences, including tough disciplinary action, and will require, when necessary, employment termination.

Practical Application
Addressing Change Resistance

1. What entrenched practices could trigger pockets of resistance to my change initiative?
2. How will I test that my messages regarding change are not ambiguous and are clearly understood at all levels?
3. How will I create discomfort in the continuation of practices that need to change?
4. What tough disciplinary action am I willing to take where resistance persists?
5. What talent and experience will I potentially lose, and how will I compensate?
6. What clear expected results and milestones have I put in place to avoid inertia triggered by resistance?
7. How well is accountability and decision authority delegated and understood?
8. How will I ensure effective execution, *inspecting what I expect,* beyond the usual written reports and PowerPoint presentations?

CHALLENGE TWO

All heads in the game

Understand business
priorities & personal impact

Directing Effort

Your team now stands engaged and excited about the vision you have created and shared with them about being the best in the industry, or the fastest growing, or the top ranking. But now what? How can you align this newly generated enthusiasm to effectively execute against clear goals? Enthusiasm can flow in many directions, and we must avoid the implications of negative energy and focus channeling into alternative and potentially conflicting agendas.

In this section of the book, we will focus on the skills necessary to create crystal-clear alignment at all levels in the organization. If well executed, alignment unleashes the power, focused energies, and talents of the team. Alignment filters and demystifies the critical few priorities that offer the highest value to your change initiative, aligning both personal and collective effort—it is realized when employees know exactly what these priorities are and how they can contribute to their execution.

Uncommon Sense

"The strangest thing about common sense is that it is not so common after all!" George Bernard Shaw once noted. Here's a perfect example:

At an executive meeting, the CFO reviewed the poor financial performance for the quarter. Noting that the full-year forecast was at risk, the CEO issued a total hiring freeze. "Let me be clear," **he said, "not a single person is to be added to our payroll until I give the go-ahead to resume recruiting. In other words, I'm putting into place a total headcount freeze. Understood?" The executives nodded, acknowledging receipt of the message and that he had been clearly understood.**

Two months later, the CEO, expecting to see zero hires, asked the head of HR for an updated headcount report. The HR executive was stunned to see that twenty new hires had taken place during the two months since the headcount freeze was introduced. Here are the justifications given by four department heads:

1. **"I had six contractors in place, which were more expensive than hiring full-time employees. I realized that if I hired them on a permanent basis and got rid of their contractor status, we would save money. I'm sure the CEO will understand."**

2. "I had already made verbal commitments to these three applicants, so I thought it would be in keeping with our company values to hire them." She also thought the CEO would understand.

3. The third executive said that a few employees left his department during the last two months so he "merely replaced them." He asserted that he had exactly the same number of employees he had before the headcount freeze began.

4. Stating that at the time of the freeze his department was 20 percent lower than budget—and lower than all the other departments—this executive felt that surely the CEO would understand because he was still the lowest in headcount relative to the budget.

To these executives, their individual interpretations of the headcount freeze made sense. When the CEO reviewed the report, however, he was not happy with the gross misalignment.

As leaders, then, assume nothing. It is better to ask seemingly obvious questions than to discover later on in the execution plan that there are numerous interpretations of the expected outcomes.

Misdirected Enthusiasm

When driving change, businesses are riddled with what I call *misdirected enthusiasm*—energy and efforts channeled into activities that, though often well intended, stall progress and distract from the achievement of goals. It would be naive to assume that the driving of alternative agendas is *always* with positive intent, but, in my experience, that has often been the case. I have seen individuals enthusiastically drive agendas in pursuit of a positive outcome for the organization while their enthusiasm was misdirected.

Here's an example that demonstrates how misdirected enthusiasm can run rampant in an organization:

After the Snapple acquisition, Cadbury Schweppes continued to acquire and assimilate key bottlers and distributors across the country, thus creating the largest fully integrated beverage business in the United States. In 2008, Cadbury Schweppes then spun off these businesses, and the new company, the Dr Pepper Snapple Group, was transformed into a public company, listed on the New York Stock Exchange. This monumental maneuver called for the integration of fundamentally different business models, diverse skill sets, entrenched practices, and conflicting mind-sets.

We faced the critical task of ensuring that the team, starting with leadership, was committed to the enterprise upon which we were about to embark.

In the midst of these challenges, some of the leaders, while extremely enthusiastic about our mission statement "to be the best beverage business in the Americas," had very different views as to how this vision should be realized. Their ideas diverged fundamentally from the original strategy that had been percolating in the minds of Cadbury Schweppes executives for twenty years. Different aspirations for the business began to emerge, creating alternative agendas, and individuals within teams found themselves in the tenuous position of having to juggle the conflicting priorities of these opposing strategies.

Misdirected enthusiasm creates inertia, dissipates energies, and squanders the valuable time and resources of key individuals. These issues can be avoided when everyone is aligned behind the right set of priorities.

Distilling the Critical Few

"When *everything* is a priority, *nothing* is a priority" is a business reality we all face. Our days, often frenetic and always dynamic, can be overwhelming as we encounter mandates that are both urgent and important.

Unfortunately, so much is *urgent* that we fail to give enough attention to the really *important*. This dilemma exists at all levels of the organization, and it is the leader's role to identify and distill the critical few top priorities behind which to align their and their team's efforts. Your people will take their cues from you, so the extent to which you ensure that the important is not lost in the tidal wave of the urgent sets the standard for others to follow. If you are flipping from one crisis to the next at the expense of key priorities, your team will model your behavior.

Distilling the critical few priorities is no easy task. It requires careful thought and the courage to say no to opportunities that, while they might add value, do not offer the highest return. Work with your leadership team to identify the key value-drivers, and determine how you will ensure that these priorities will be supported at all levels of the organization.

The Dr Pepper Snapple Call to ACTION Campaign: Establishing Priorities

For Dr Pepper Snapple, identifying top priorities proved relatively easy. When they announced they would take the company public, a primary goal was to prepare a deck for use in investor presentations. Five of the largest long-term, value-creating opportunities for the organization were distilled and featured in a campaign named Call to ACTION. These priorities became the focus areas for all employees, in every function of the organization.

To date, though the tactics may vary from year to year, the priorities of the Call to ACTION campaign remain the same:

Be aware that one function or division alone cannot achieve these types of priorities. They demand exceptional cross-functional collaboration in their design and execution. This consistency of focus and messaging has proven extremely powerful for both engagement and alignment.

Though we all experience the natural, inherent tensions that exist between functions, successful companies facilitate a constructive conflict through collaborative processes that unleash the value inherent within those tensions. They identify business priorities that span across different strata within the organization and discover the full potential of the team and the types of priorities that meet the criteria needed.

Thoroughly Communicate the What

Once you have identified and agreed upon your top priorities, you can never overcommunicate them. When you think you are becoming redundant and repetitive, your job as communicator has only just begun. Let me illustrate this with an analogy: Imagine you are standing at a crossroad and a car accident occurs in front of you. I'm sure that though they observed the same accident, witness accounts would vary. Whether their view was from north, east, south, or west, or they were looking from the window of a high-rise building, their perspectives and interpretations of the accident would be measurably different.

You need to repeat your messages on *what* to focus on from every possible angle and viewpoint. In all cases, put yourself in the shoes of the recipient of your message. Your message needs to be consistent yet tailored for different audiences at different times within the organization. Make use of every possible method of communication, and allow the creativity of your people to emerge. Engage them in how the message is to be communicated. Particularly when you are communicating important messages, a comprehensive approach will strengthen alignment behind a common understanding of the agenda and priorities, as well as progressively erode misinterpretation.

As you launch your change agenda, adopt some of the fundamentals that marketing adopts when launching a brand, product, or service:

- How will you ensure that the "product offering" connects with your target market?
- What key brand attributes do you need to communicate with clarity and creativity?

- How will you ensure that your message is heard above the clutter of all the communications that employees are bombarded with?

In the retail business, a key ingredient to success is capturing the best possible "share of shelf space." In change communication, your goal is to capture the best possible "share of mind"—keeping your change agenda front and center and effectively stated in all communications.

Not all leaders are good communicators; some will need a translator to help ensure that their communications achieve their desired outcomes.

A bright leader with whom I once worked possessed an incredible intellect—his ability to grasp and interpret complex situations was remarkable. He could process terabytes of data per second, yet it was as if this computer-like mind was attached to a dot-matrix printer. His ability to communicate his thoughts with others was sorely lacking, often riddled with innuendos, inferences, and ambiguities. We had to surround him with those who could translate his messages so that all employees in the organization could understand and respond appropriately.

Always keep the big picture in mind. While team members will have interpretations biased by their own frames of reference, knowledge, and personal interests, you have to be able to "helicopter" over the scene. This enables you to monitor different perspectives and interpretations of the agenda and to direct future communications in order to strengthen alignment.

Guiding Principles— Guiding the How of Execution

We know that driving meaningful change is always a venture into the unknown. As a consequence, even the best-planned change agendas can be messy at times. But change need not be—and should not be— disorganized and chaotic. Unnecessary disruption during change draws people into activities that do not contribute meaningfully to the change effort. Incessant disruption distracts focus and stifles momentum.

We can mitigate the inherent disruption of change by agreeing to a set of "guiding principles." Prior to embarking on a change initiative, it is essential to develop and agree upon this set of principles that all decision makers will adhere to during the change process. Guiding principles create a framework and set of disciplines that anchor decision making. This is particularly important when decisions need to be made about employees and their roles going forward, or when time schedules are tight and consulting on all decisions is impractical.

Guiding principles, then, enable leaders to delegate decision authority to maintain the momentum of change while avoiding disruptive precedents set by misaligned decisions.

When developing guiding principles, it is also important that the consequences of these decisions are fully understood at all levels of the organization and that leaders understand their obligation to operate consistently within these approved principles. If there are to be any exceptions (which there normally are), specify under what circumstances these will be entertained, how they will be reviewed, and who will make the final decision.

As leaders, the management of these decisions must bear scrutiny. By this I don't mean that everyone must like the decisions you make, but rather that you have an objective rationale for the decisions made and that you can present your rationale confidently to all employees, regardless of their roles or levels in the company.

Consistency in your handling of these situations and an open communication regarding the guiding principles demonstrate equity in your approach. How you handle these people-decisions is even more important to those who remain on the team going forward than to those who leave the company during organizational change. After all, those who remain form the team that will help you achieve your future goals, and how fairly and consistently you treated their departing colleagues will influence their ongoing commitment to your leadership.

Some years ago, I witnessed the significant inertia and disruption created by the absence of guiding principles during a major change undertaking.

The well-meaning HR leader, in an attempt to please all those disrupted by change, began accommodating unique needs. Staff members approached him for one-on-one meetings, at which they negotiated personal accommodations based on their particular circumstances and expectations. Within a very short period of time, employees were comparing the respective unique offers they had secured. Now the cherry-picking negotiation began: "Why am I expected to relocate and John is not?" No clear answer that could bear scrutiny. "Why can she get a relocation allowance that includes three house-hunting trips and I don't?" No objective criteria for the decision. "Why does he keep his job title and I must change mine?" No clear guidelines on job titles were agreed.

This soon became a feeding frenzy, slowing down integration as the leaders spent valuable time untangling this mess. The really

painful part was that the credibility of leadership took a serious blow. They were caught in defensive mode, not having had time as a team to develop a united approach to the situations brought about by the ripple effects of change. They had neither prepared effective responses nor carefully considered the implications of the decisions they had to make to rectify the situation. Needless to say, the restructuring costs allocated for the project were sorely insufficient.

So it is essential that we identify and agree on the guiding principles with our guiding coalition and leadership *before* the change initiative gets underway. Well-defined guiding principles will confirm:

- That the disruption inherent in change will be reduced.
- That the implications of change are better understood.
- That leadership will execute change with consistency.
- That exceptions to the guiding principles will bear scrutiny.

The Grand Canyon Effect

Once change is underway, it is easy for leaders to become so engrossed in the details of the agenda that the larger perspective of the initiative is lost. Leaders must retain their holistic perspective, being vigilant at identifying any hairline cracks in employee engagement and alignment. An inappropriate or misinterpreted action or event can quickly become a war story, cascading deep into the organization, creating doubt, speculation, and skepticism surrounding your change agenda. Left unattended, as individuals add their interpretations to events, one hairline crack, within a short period of time, can expand into a grand canyon. These occurrences need to be identified and addressed quickly to maintain change momentum and stop the erosion of alignment.

The
Grand Canyon
Effect

The best way to illustrate this phenomenon is to share a story with you.

A senior executive of a major beverage business was adamant that a newly developed soft drink could compete head-to-head with the best-selling cola brand. His research and development team had developed a cola concentrate that could be used with home carbonating machines to create a cola drink that he believed could take market share from the competitor. In theory, this was not a bad idea, and given recent technology advancements, an idea likely ahead of its time.

The marketing team was instructed to conduct a feasibility study and present their findings to the leadership team.

After thorough analysis, the team delivered a well-structured presentation to the leadership team in the boardroom, clearly demonstrating that the product would struggle to gain traction in the market—a successful launch would require a significantly higher financial investment than the projected future sales volume could justify.

The senior executive who had germinated the idea was clearly frustrated: "I need people around this table who have the courage to take on the giants. Everyone knows that Marketing can make numbers and stats say anything they want. Rework your results, and let's make this a success."

The meeting adjourned, and the senior executive left the room. Raising his eyebrows, the marketing vice president muttered, "OK, we'll distort the numbers. Let's go create an outcome that will make this wacky product work!" A number of people overheard his comment and chuckled.

Within a few months, it was clear that the product was a failure. During a visit to a retail store, the VP of the marketing team ran into a junior sales merchandiser from the company, who then remarked, "So, how is the boss's new wacky product doing?" He smiled, waiting for a response.

The marketing VP was taken aback by the overt criticism of a senior executive by this junior employee. How had he heard about this comment made in the company's boardroom, and what made him believe it was OK to criticize the senior executive in front of him?

It was clear that this "war story" had cascaded through the organization. This merchandiser had been emboldened by his manager, who in turn had been bolstered by his manager to repeat this derisive comment. Ultimately, those counterproductive words had trickled through the entire organization, giving the statement a legitimacy that tainted everyone with a negativity that undermined commitment to the new product. This widening chasm sealed the demise of the product.

Leadership at all levels must proceed with one voice—a united commitment to a course of action that will retain crystal-clear alignment. If not, hairline fractures will result in widening dissent, undermining your ability to drive effective change.

Practical Application
Directing Effort

Uncommon Sense

For change initiatives that you are leading, what assumptions are you making about your people's understanding of:

1. Timing—what needs to be done by when?
2. Standards—what does "great" look like?
3. Accountabilities—who is accountable for what?

Misdirected Enthusiasm

1. What alternative agendas are being driven by groups or individuals within your team?
2. What resources are being dissipated due to misdirected effort?

Distilling and Communicating the Critical Few

What are the few most critical focus areas that, if executed effectively, will:

1. Offer the highest value-creating opportunity for the business?
2. Move the organization significantly toward the realization of its goal/vision?
3. Leverage the power of cross-functional collaboration?
4. Help create sustainable competitive advantage?

Thoroughly Communicate the *What*

In today's world of communication overload, consider the following challenges:

1. How will you define these focus areas, measure them, and monitor them?

2. How are you going to communicate these priorities in a manner that is understandable to all employees?

3. How will you get people to focus their attention on these priorities?

4. How will you capture "share of mind"?

5. What are the best communication methods to connect with your target audience?

6. How will you reinforce the messages with healthy repetition, without being boring?

7. How will you build the brand awareness of the idea or agenda?

Guiding Principles

Consider the following people-decisions requiring guiding principles during your change:

1. Will you relocate staff? If so, at what job levels? What is the value of the relocation package? Does it differ from role to role?

2. Rather than relocate, can individuals work remotely?

3. Will compensation for individuals be grandfathered if they accept a different role?

4. What severance package will you offer? Under what circumstances?

5. Who will have the final say on the selection of candidates?

6. Will you adjust structure to accommodate a particular skill set?

The Grand Canyon Effect

Successful engagement is at risk when even a hairline crack in commitment appears at the senior levels of an organization. If left unaddressed, these hairline cracks can become chasms that kill momentum.

1. What hairline cracks in engagement have you yet to address?
2. How can healthy constructive contention help you wrestle through optional approaches to a business issue or opportunity?
3. Having decided upon a course of action, have you communicated the unwavering commitment that you expect from all members of the team? What specifically do you need them to do to demonstrate this commitment?

Shaping New Behaviors

As products of our environment, we are shaped by the norms we have embraced, adapted to, or rejected. Sometimes we are beneficiaries, sometimes victims, but influenced nonetheless.

In the newly formed Dr Pepper Snapple Group, many members of the integrated team saw the world from insular perspectives. These perspectives had been built over many years of experience, whether within the silos of a bottler or franchisor, in businesses that were family owned, held by private equity, or part of an international company.

In the business environment, we can become so entrenched in the way we do things that our behaviors define us and become filters through which we evaluate the actions of others.

Let's explore this by returning to our Dr Pepper Snapple story:

The franchise and bottling operation business models were so fundamentally different that they shared little common ground other than being in the soft drink industry. The palpable tension and animosity between the groups had been entrenched over years of conflict as both parties tried to impart onto each other the rising costs within the value chain. The on-shelf price of a can of soda had remained virtually unchanged for ten years, while costs of raw materials, packaging, labor, and transportation had risen consistently each year. Retailers were demanding greater profitability from every square inch of shelf space in their stores. Profit margins of bottlers had been under tremendous pressure for years. As a consequence, relationships had been less than cordial. Bringing these teams together to create one united organization created significant challenges. Bottlers saw the franchise team as squanderers—wasting valuable resources on corporate initiatives that from their perspective added little value; the franchise team saw the bottlers as so tactical that they were unwilling to invest in brand equity or infrastructure, thus compromising brand quality and product distribution.

Who was right? Who was wrong? As I mentioned in the introduction to mobilization, your leadership challenge is to create, manage, and leverage constructive contention in an environment where those with opposing arguments approach conflict with an assumption of positive intent. It is within this environment of healthy conflict that you are able to create dynamic and holistic solutions to business challenges.

Osmosis

To shape new behaviors, a leader must explore the flaws and strengths within their team's current realities and provide it with the tools to form new realities.

In high school, I was fascinated by science experiments that demonstrated osmosis—"the movement of molecules through a partially permeable membrane in a direction that leads to equalization of concentration."

This process often occurs in the workplace. Through a form of osmosis, norms and standards are continually reshaped to form a new normal. Moving in a direction that leads to equalization, tension reduces through compromise. The healthy competitive edge that was once maintained through constructive contention insidiously erodes. People become removed from other realities, myopically judging performance only against the standards with which they have become familiar and comfortable—often oblivious to the subtleties of these shifts over time. They adapt and conform to their environments and pressure others to do the same.

Osmosis alters us with a gradual yet deliberate process. In driving fundamental change, we must create new realities that align the priorities and activities of our people to stretch themselves in the pursuit of goals that are beyond their current circumstances.

Unless we are beyond learning and new discovery, we must courageously accept the insight from Sir Arthur Conan Doyle, who wrote that "mediocrity knows nothing higher than itself." We don't know what we don't know, and this lack of exposure forms blind spots that lead to a mediocre view of what "great" could look like.

In today's dynamic business environment, driving competitive advantage requires a reversing of the osmosis process that has shaped our people's views of excellence and of what is achievable.

Here is a story that illustrates this principle:

In the spice manufacturing division of a company I worked for in South Africa, I was invited to inspect the new standards that technicians had implemented in their maintenance department. Since I was the executive sponsor and champion of the Quality Circles Program we were implementing at the time, the team was excited to show me how they had successfully transformed their work environment in zealous pursuit of our quality initiative. With difficulty, I managed to disguise my disappointment in what I saw that day: while the improvement was significant compared to the original state of disarray, the standards were nowhere near where they needed to be for a food manufacturing environment.

Some thought we were faced with a lack of commitment to our quality campaign. On the contrary, these employees were passionately committed to the program, but their limited perspective of what "great" could look like influenced their actions. They were products of their environments—shaped by the standards to which they had become accustomed. They did not know what they did not know.

Our challenge was to expose them to an environment in which exceptionally higher quality standards were understood and well embedded, one that could help them envision a picture of a preferred future state.

I knew the perfect environment. Our company had entered into a partnership with a chicken-processing company that had redefined the meaning of excellence in its industry.

Their exceptional focus on quality began after they had endured a disastrous spread of bird flu that had virtually wiped out their entire chicken inventory. As a consequence of this event that had almost bankrupted their business, they implemented breakthrough standards of quality and hygiene, setting new industry benchmarks.

I wanted our maintenance technicians to be exposed to this standard of excellence, so we arranged for a visit and flew across the country with four of our technicians to visit the maintenance department of the chicken processing company. It was in pristine condition. Every technician in the department radiated pride in the environment they had created and in the machinery they so meticulously maintained. The refrigeration compressor units resembled the gleaming engines of a biker's beloved Harley Davidson rather than industrial machinery. These units had been fully depreciated, yet they continued to perform superbly due to the outstanding preventive maintenance performed by a team of very proud technicians. The experience had a profound impact on our technicians and indelibly implanted in their minds a new reality of what was possible. On our return flight, they eagerly developed plans to mirror the magnificent environment they had just experienced and to begin transforming their own maintenance shop as soon as possible.

Three months later, I was asked to revisit their newly transformed workshop. I was delighted with the results and proud of the team's accomplishments.

The visualization of a new reality had inspired in them a fundamental rethink of what was possible.

In my career, I have moved back and forth between line functions, support functions, operational roles, and corporate roles. Whenever I moved into a support or corporate role, I made a conscious effort to remain in touch with the reality of the customer-facing part of the business. I strived to remain as close as possible to the frontline of the organization, where the real business of making, selling, and distributing products and services occurs. Unfortunately, despite my best efforts, over time, I began to unconsciously adapt to my environment. Osmosis gradually eroded my understanding of frontline business realities.

This subtle and innocuous creep of osmosis permeates us all. We become tainted by the behaviors and norms that surround us, and, before we realize it, our thinking and actions adjust accordingly.

This is analogous to an experience I had as a student sharing accommodations with five other young men. Among other areas in the house, the refrigerator was a reflection of our undomesticated proclivities. One day, I was preparing a sandwich and found half an unwrapped onion sitting next to a stick of unwrapped butter. I spread some of the butter onto my bread, added a healthy dollop of strawberry preserve, and took a huge bite. The taste was disgusting. While the butter looked like butter and spread like butter, it tasted like onion. Having been exposed too long to the raw onion in the refrigerator, the butter had been tainted.

We, too, become tainted by what we deem to be the accepted practices around us—we are victims of osmosis and the onion effect. It is no surprise, then, that sometimes, driving meaningful change in organizations requires the injection of new talent—people who can bring fresh perspectives.

The first step in any change undertaking is to acknowledge that we *need* to change. Sometimes we are so comfortable and entrenched in our practices that we are oblivious to higher standards around us, eroding our ability to compete. Recognizing that our perceived competency is not what we believe it to be is often a rude awakening, but it is a critical step in enabling real change to occur.

In the illustration below, we see the journey of change that we must lead our people through.

Embracing Change
The Learning Journey

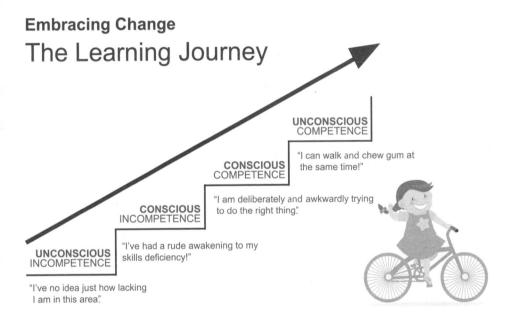

As you work through this framework, remember yourself as a young child learning to ride a bicycle. Initially, you had no idea just how incompetent you were at this activity. Perhaps you saw your older sibling riding around with ease, and you were convinced that you, too, could achieve the same effortlessly. You did not know what you did not know. You were unconscious of your incompetence.

Then your day came. You got onto the saddle and sped off, only to meet the realities of balance and gravity. Suddenly, you became very conscious of your cycling incompetence. At that point, the learning process began as you awkwardly, simultaneously, and with great determination concentrated on balance, steering, pedaling, and braking. You were being very conscious in your efforts to be competent—the consequence of failure being a tumble and potential bruising.

Over time, your competence grew and, with that, your confidence. Cycling soon became second nature, a motor skill. You became unconsciously competent, able to chat to your friends while cycling, even taking your hands off the handlebars.

This is the journey of change that you, as a leader, will need to help your team travel through, giving them needed support along the way.

Shattering Titles and Labels

Too often, the job titles and labels we ascribe to positions, processes, and functions inaccurately describe what actually takes place and what individuals are truly accountable for. The standardization of job titles evolved to support HR job evaluation processes that enabled the generic matching of jobs across industries. This is helpful for the development of salary comparison data, but, unfortunately, titles often inappropriately shape what people do, what they think they should do, and how important they believe they are.

Change agendas offer us the opportunity to fundamentally rethink roles and titles. In fact, many companies are now shattering locked-in and entrenched norms associated with job titles. Words are powerful and can invoke very specific interpretations. As you revisit titles, think of inspiring words that you can infuse into them in order to positively motivate employees and affect customers. Think of the benefits that the company and the team would enjoy as a consequence of the role being executed effectively. For example, a recruitment officer might be called a talent scout; an HR generalist, a culture champion; a receptionist, a leader of first impressions. And though the title may be manager (which presumes functions such as planning, organizing, controlling, and directing), isn't every manager also a coach? When we accurately describe their roles, titles may favorably shift perceptions for all concerned.

I have the privilege of supporting My Possibilities (www .MyPossibilities.org), a nonprofit organization dedicated to the continued education and development of adults with cognitive challenges. Founded in 2008 by my wife, Charmaine Solomon, this operation is a resounding success and an excellent example of what can be achieved when a team of dedicated individuals break the mold and fundamentally redefine previously entrenched views of what is possible for adults with special needs.

Yet so many nonprofits struggle to keep their doors open despite the heart-wrenching needs they want so desperately to meet. I believe that part of the problem has to do with how so many people in nonprofit organizations perceive their roles. I've spoken to numerous individuals who pursue employment in the nonprofit field, and, all too often, I've heard comments like:

- I chose nonprofit because it is less demanding than for-profit organizations.
- Corporate employment is too competitive and aggressive for me.
- I don't want the pressures I would have if I worked in the business world.
- We do our best, but it all depends on what we can get through charitable gifts.

The term nonprofit can be misleading. Fulfilling the noble visions of so many nonprofit organizations calls for significant funding, which requires excellent business capabilities and a team that is as driven as those in for-profit organizations.

At My Possibilities, the team shows exceptional leadership by shattering titles and labels. The adults with special needs are affectionately known as HIPsters—Hugely Important People—and that's how they are treated by all involved. My Possibilities developed the following mission statement that fundamentally defines their purpose and governs their every action:

MY POSSIBILITIES

LEARN LIVE GROW

"We courageously and relentlessly pursue
the full, untapped possibilities
of our Hugely Important People,
making every day count!"

This statement drives all initiatives, and it is the yardstick by which they measure all activities. Whether planning for the future, hiring staff, or building capabilities, the driving question at My Possibilities is always "Do our plans help us courageously and relentlessly pursue the full, untapped possibilities of our HIPsters?" By redefining its labels and purpose, My Possibilities has created a significant, positive shift in the mind-sets and behaviors among all who are involved in the program.

My Possibilities staff do not refer to themselves as a nonprofit organization, but rather as a "for-cause enterprise"—far more important than, and as demanding as, any for-profit organization.

Make the How Simple

One of the most critical roles of the person at the head of an organization is to define and embed the culture. There are occasions when, in pursuit of the latest trends, HR may attempt to imbue cultural norms into an organization. When these newly introduced ideas do not represent the natural behavior of the person leading the company or division, such efforts will fail. We've already noted that people take their cues and their clues from their leaders. If no clear alignment between the leader's spoken words and actions exists, the promoted behaviors will fail to gain traction or credibility.

The Dr Pepper Snapple Call to ACTION Campaign: Establishing Core Behaviors

With the formation of the Dr Pepper Snapple company, we seized the opportunity to build upon the Call to ACTION priorities and add core behaviors to the program.

In the newly formed Dr Pepper Snapple, the strife between bottlers and franchisors was still festering, albeit now in one family. Our CEO, Larry Young, became increasingly frustrated with counterproductive behavior patterns that kept surfacing. He and I knew that successful integration of these disparate businesses depended upon our ability to shape and embed a new set of behaviors that would enable collaboration across over two hundred locations. As his translator, Larry Young expected me to create and implement pragmatic approaches that would either change the behaviors or "change the people." My initial textbook approach was not a success.

Though I had access to exploratory tools—i.e., in-depth research, outside consultants—I soon realized that the best resource was Larry Young himself. After thirty-five years of soft drink industry experience, rising from the role of a delivery driver, our CEO knew exactly which behaviors were counterproductive and which drove success in this business.

My challenge as translator was to extract from his experience and observations a set of behaviors behind which we would align the organization and that would enable the execution of the five priorities already established in 2008 (see chapter 4, "The Dr Pepper Snapple Call to ACTION Campaign: Setting Priorities"). After several interviews with Larry, the communications team and I were able to distill six core behaviors, which, if embedded in the organization, would effectively counter the ingrained unproductive behavior patterns.

To simplify the communication of these new behaviors, we created the acronym ACTION:

- **A**ccountable. Say what you're going to do; do what you say.
- **C**ustomer Centric. Focus on customers' and consumers' needs.
- **T**ransparent and Honest. Share knowledge and information openly; no hidden agendas.
- **I**nspect What We Expect. Define your expectations; inspect progress and results.
- **O**wn Decisions. Boldly and courageously make decisions with facts and input.
- **N**o Blame Fixing. The solution begins with me.

To bring these behaviors to life and to effect continuity, we implemented the following processes:

1. ACTION behavior visuals were displayed in every location of the business, leveraging every possible communication forum to reinforce these behaviors.
2. The ACTION behaviors were included into the performance management system, ensuring that the demonstration of these behaviors became an important dimension of overall performance evaluation.
3. On-the-spot ACTION Awards, in the form of gift cards, were made available to managers across the organization. This enabled them to "catch others doing things right," immediately recognizing displays of the new expected behaviors.
4. Sizeable ACTION Hero Awards were presented annually to a dozen employees who over the previous year had best demonstrated the ACTION behaviors in the execution of their duties. The twelve recipients were identified through a selection process and invited to a prestigious event at which they were recognized and awarded meaningful stock grants.

These behaviors were embedded into the day-to-day activities of twenty thousand Dr Pepper Snapple employees. Leaders, in particular, were expected to be ambassadors of the ACTION behaviors, clearly leading by example. Individuals who acted contrary to these behaviors, regardless of tenure, seniority, or expertise, were held accountable for their actions.

In 2008, we integrated the Dr Pepper priorities and the ACTION behaviors into a single-page document that defined *what* and *how* the business would succeed. That document has remained consistent for over seven years. There is real beauty in this simplicity. These behaviors are easily remembered and have stood the test of time.

New ACTION behaviors

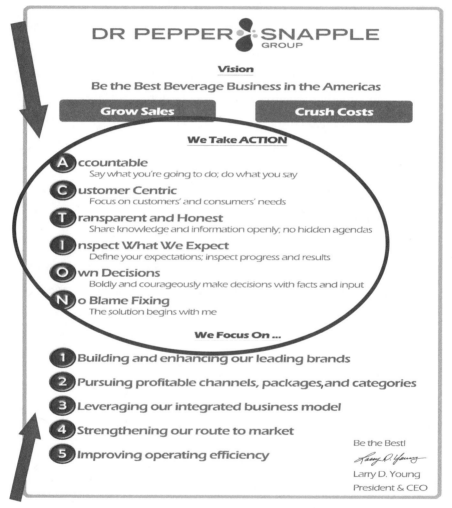

DR PEPPER SNAPPLE GROUP

Vision
Be the Best Beverage Business in the Americas

Grow Sales   **Crush Costs**

We Take ACTION

Accountable
Say what you're going to do; do what you say

Customer Centric
Focus on customers' and consumers' needs

Transparent and Honest
Share knowledge and information openly; no hidden agendas

Inspect What We Expect
Define your expectations; inspect progress and results

Own Decisions
Boldly and courageously make decisions with facts and input

No Blame Fixing
The solution begins with me

We Focus On ...

1 Building and enhancing our leading brands

2 Pursuing profitable channels, packages, and categories

3 Leveraging our integrated business model

4 Strengthening our route to market

5 Improving operating efficiency

Be the Best!

Larry D. Young
President & CEO

To enable new priorities

Often, leaders assume that, given time, the right behaviors will emerge, or they struggle to clearly articulate the behaviors that will drive performance. Start by describing from your own experience what has made teams successful in the past and what you have seen people do that has undermined team effectiveness. Engage your translator—someone who can give you feedback—elicit input from others, and help distill your thinking into a handful of clearly defined, easily understandable behaviors. These expected behaviors will need to be meaningful to employees throughout the organization. Relentlessly seize every opportunity to recognize appropriate behaviors and consistently redirect the behaviors of those that act contrary to these new expectations. In shaping behaviors, systematically remove any ambiguity of translation so that clear directives are never misconstrued as suggestions or subject to personal interpretations.

From the boardroom to the shop floor, weaving expected behaviors into the day-to-day fabric of a business brings them to life and ensures their relevance throughout your business.

Practical Application
Shaping New Behaviors

Osmosis, Titles, and Labels

As you reflect on the fundamental changes you desire to drive, consider the following:

1. Has osmosis clouded your judgment and the judgment of your team?
2. Reflect on your own behaviors—what have you come to tolerate as acceptable?
3. How have these norms changed and shaped over time? Why?
4. What influence have your bosses, peers, staff, and surroundings had on your behaviors?
5. How entrenched have you become in these new views of reality?
6. What can you do to ensure that you and your team stay in touch with the frontline realities of your organization?
7. How will you and your team keep abreast of what "new" is happening around you in order to disrupt norms embedded by myopia?
8. What preconceptions created by labels and titles do you need to shatter?

Making the How Simple

For the successful implementation of your change agenda, consider the following:

1. What are the critical few behaviors that must be demonstrated deep in your organization?

2. What entrenched behaviors must change?
3. What plans do you have to drive this behavior change?
4. What tough people-situations will you need to confront in order to change the behaviors of key influencers?
5. How will these behaviors be translated into the day-to-day actions of all employees?
6. What consequences (positive and negative) will you link to expected behaviors?

Demystifying the Agenda

Once you have defined the expected behaviors to support the change, you will need to translate the business strategies into the domain of all employees—they will need to understand the initiatives' relevance to them in order to establish a connection with the agenda and to align behind it. In this chapter, we will discuss the power of using visuals to demystify business strategies and tactics, and how we can create cross-functional forums that allow employees to work together to translate change priorities into their day-to-day worlds:

First, we will explore the use of visuals to describe the stages ahead and what we need to focus our efforts against.

Next, we will examine how we can create visuals to monitor progress against tactics within our strategic priorities.

In closing the chapter, we will discuss the power of collaborative, cross-functional workshops in the enabling of effective execution.

THE POWER OF VISUALS
Visual Representation of the Journey

There is truth in the age-old saying "A picture tells a thousand words." There are few communication tools more powerful than a visual representation of the key elements of a strategy. This is especially true when those accountable for executing the strategy are actively involved in creating the visual. I have seen leaders in diverse businesses, countries, and cultures use employee-developed visuals to effectively communicate and reinforce important strategies, tactics, and messages. When individuals are involved in this process, they develop a strong commitment to deliver against the strategy. Involvement magnifies commitment.

When we launched the Call to ACTION campaign in 2008, this is precisely the approach we used. We knew that our first challenge would be to build a common understanding of the opportunities created by the integration of franchising and bottling operations. We expected that the twenty thousand employees, spread over more than two hundred locations across the United States, Canada, and Mexico, would have many different views about the future of the newly formed company and how we would get there.

We needed to describe our future and the priorities we would highlight in a way that would build common understanding and commitment. This had to be executed in a manner that would bridge cultural and language barriers, as well as help break some of the biases toward entrenched business models and perceived value drivers. The ultimate goals were to defy the odds and outperform our competitors, gain market share, and delight shareholders—no small task.

Visual Representation of the Overall Strategy: Our "Road Map to Success"

The first critical component of the process was to create a visual representation of the journey we were undertaking as a team. This visual, known as the "Road Map to Success," was developed through a series of discussions with teams of cross-functional employees at all levels of the organization. We explored the progression of our soft drink brands from their inception to their consumption, taking time to understand the entire process, the roles of different functions, and the challenges and opportunities along the way.

To gain their input and support, we asked key internal stakeholders to examine the visual before making it available to leaders across the organization. Once it was finalized, leaders, using a common script, reviewed the road map with their teams and addressed its relevance to every employee.

The Road Map to Success helped us:

- Involve all levels of the organization in our initiative.
- Understand the functional and process interdependencies.
- Recognize the contributions of previously undervalued functions.
- Graphically visualize a broad overview of the undertaking.
- Achieve a sense of ownership, because the creation of the road map was a collaborative effort.

Road Map to Success

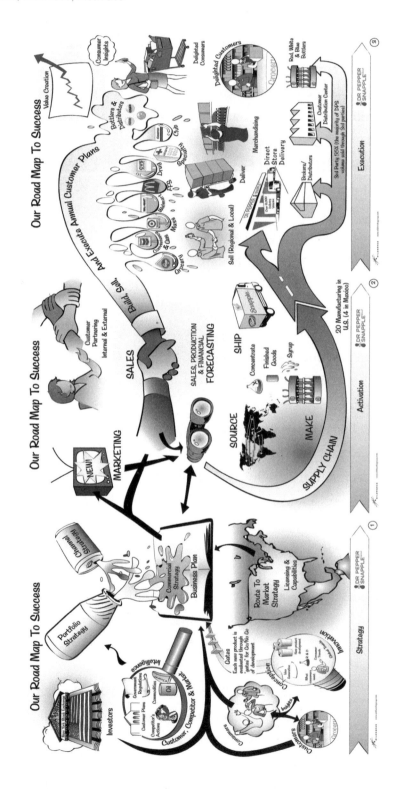

Visual Representation of Key Strategies and Tactics

It is difficult to comprehend how we can compete effectively in a business environment in which 95 percent of employees are either unaware of or have little understanding of their company's strategies (Kaplan & Norton 2005). Most employees do not perceive how their everyday activities impact their organizations.

After presenting a visual representation of the journey, then, the second component of the process is to visually represent the key elements within the strategic priorities. Let's once again use Dr Pepper Snapple's ACTION campaign to address this point.

We initiated a series of meetings with the executives most accountable for the respective outcomes of each of the five priorities. Our objective was to identify a handful of critically important tactics that, if executed effectively, would provide the greatest contribution to the success of each strategic priority.

With this input, we created a visual representation of each strategy along with its required critical tactics. Once again, these visuals were refined through a collaborative process, eliciting cross-functional input from employees deep within the organization.

What did these five visuals achieve?

- First and foremost, the process forced executives to think carefully about and commit to the critical few tactics to focus on for the execution of each strategy.
- The visuals served as a storyboard to describe the core components of each strategic priority.
- They aligned all employees behind the tactics necessary to execute the five strategic priorities.

- Icons within the visuals helped build a common language across the business.

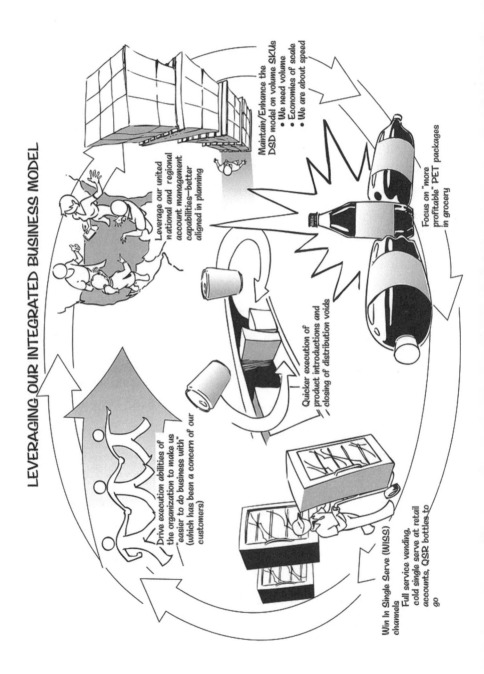

LEVERAGING OUR INTEGRATED BUSINESS MODEL

Maintain/Enhance the DSD model on volume SKUs
• We need volume
• Economies of scale
• We are about speed

Focus on "more profitable" PET packages in grocery

Leverage our united national and regional account management capabilities—better aligned in planning

Quicker execution of product introductions and closing of distribution voids

Drive execution abilities of the organization to make us easier to do business with" (which has been a concern of our customers)

Win In Single Serve (WISS) channels
Full service vending, cold single serve at retail accounts, QSR bottles to go

Visual Representation to Monitor Progress against Tactics

Finally, the third component of the process is to use visuals to monitor and communicate progress against agreed-upon tactics within the strategic priorities. This helps to maintain focus, strengthen cross-functional effort, and empower the team by giving members a tool to help control outcomes.

Example 1—Forecast Accuracy

Bottler and distributor operations bring great strength to an integrated business model—strengths that a franchisor does not have. However, these operations also bring to the business the burden of significant working capital.

Competing in the fast-moving consumer business of soft drinks calls for continual innovation and a proliferation of Stock Keeping Units (SKUs). Dr Pepper Snapple had literally hundreds of millions of dollars tied up in working capital, finished goods, raw materials, and packaging across the country. This emerged as a real opportunity to drive out waste. We set a goal to increase forecast accuracy by 10 percent.

No single function could achieve this goal independently. Finance, production, sales, and marketing needed to sacrifice their own personal forecasts on the altar of collaboration in order to build one forecast that all would believe in, focus on, and execute against.

The Call to ACTION campaign was extraordinarily powerful in driving constructive contention and building united cross-functional commitment to common goals. For this particular goal, a simple icon was incorporated into our strategy maps and became synonymous with the challenge of improving forecast accuracy:

This icon became a simple but effective reminder of needed focus and facilitated visual reporting on progress. Through constant monitoring and powerful collaboration, the team successfully freed up millions of dollars previously tied up in working capital. Not only did the company benefit from the direct interest savings, it could now redirect the freed-up resources to higher value opportunities. With lower inventory levels, the team also increased customer service levels.

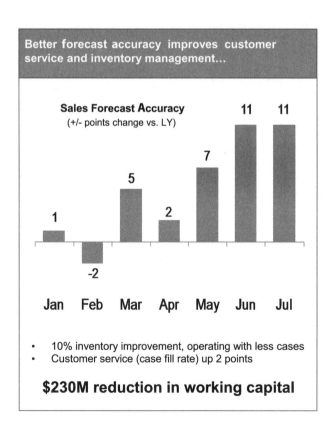

Every change initiative needs a banner or two that enables everyone from floor sweeper to CEO to become practically involved. "Crushing Costs" became a mantra, enabling twenty thousand Dr Pepper Snapple employees to contribute directly to this important project. In order to compete to win against the cola giants, Dr Pepper Snapple had to run a lean operation. The Crushing Costs visual below became a reminder of this priority and was used to effectively monitor progress, communicate results, and recognize heroes.

Example 2—Product Loss

Visuals helped build momentum behind another significant cross-functional Call to ACTION initiative: the crushing costs associated with product loss. These losses—a result of obsolescence (products that are beyond their best-by dates), breakage (products that are damaged in warehousing or transit), and shrinkage (the pilferage that occurs in the delivery process from manufacturing to the retail store shelf)—required meaningful collaboration and joint problem solving between the sales, marketing, manufacturing, warehousing, distribution, and finance departments. Some of the operations were experiencing breakage and shrinkage costs that were twice as high as the industry average. This offered a clear opportunity to significantly crush costs through cross-functional teamwork. We used the following image to communicate the message, and it became synonymous with the initiative to significantly reduce obsolescence, breakage, and shrinkage.

Within a few years, the cost was reduced to well below industry average and saved the company millions of dollars in reduced operating expenses.

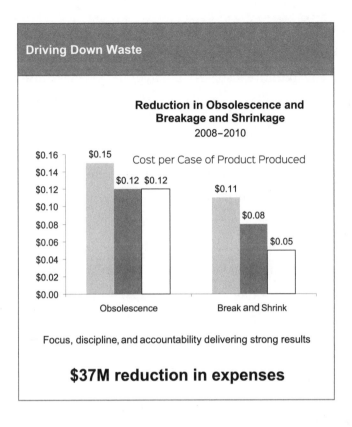

Consider how the visual representation of your business's journey, your strategies, and your tactics can contribute to higher degrees of engagement and alignment of employees deep within your organization.

THE POWER OF CROSS-FUNCTIONAL WORKSHOPS

To support unmistakable alignment at this stage, we have already armed ourselves with:

1. well-defined strategic priorities;
2. understandable expected behaviors;
3. a collaborative visual roadmap of the journey ahead; and
4. the translation of strategic priorities into critical tactics for execution.

Now alignment begins to happen, and the process of positive osmosis can occur. But osmosis can be slow, and, when speed is a factor, a more deliberate intervention is required.

We need to inject a catalyst—something that will accelerate the demystifying of the agenda and the translation of priorities into the day-to-day worlds of *all* employees. Cross-functional workshops—forums that allow employees to work together to discuss, translate, and activate strategies through their collective efforts—can be powerful motivators. They worked extremely well for Dr Pepper Snapple.

Cross-Functional Workshops

These workshops included employees from diverse functions and operations who would then have the opportunity to identify problems and commit to take action. Held in business units and offices across the United States, Canada, and Mexico, the workshops focused on the ACTION behaviors, the "Roadmap to Success," and the five strategies and tactics. The process started with senior leadership and was systematically cascaded throughout the organization. Over a period of twelve months, more than seven thousand salaried employees were engaged in workshops designed to demystify the strategies and build an understanding of the business processes. (A similar process was used for the thirteen thousand critically important frontline employees. See chapter 10.)

To constructively challenge every participant, the CEO delivered this directive in the opening video for the workshop: "After this workshop, when I see you, I will ask you what you are now doing *differently* to take action, and I invite you to ask me the same question." Word soon spread that this expectation was real. The CEO's challenge helped strengthen the focus of these workshops—to create our new, fully integrated business.

Cross-functionality in every Call to ACTION workshop became the hallmark. Teams of twenty-five to thirty employees from different functions reviewed and discussed the key strategies and built a common understanding of the undertaking ahead. Together, they wrestled with challenges and discovered creative and unique ways of adding value. When a merchandising branch manager and a corporate internal auditor spent a day together discussing strategy, tactics, and expected behaviors, their appreciation of each other's role—and the business—grew exponentially.

Most importantly, during these cross-functional discussions, participants identified and committed to a set of personal goals. To realize these goals, they outlined the actions they would take within their areas of responsibility to contribute toward the implementation of the strategic tactics. Key to these commitments was the realization and acknowledgment of needed changes in behavior in order to unlock value in the integrated business model.

Why were these Call to ACTION workshops critical to the change process?

- They started at the top of the organization and were systematically cascaded.
- No employee was excluded.

- Teams were cross-functional by design, thus building an appreciation of differing contributions to success.
- They helped break down myopic and distorted views of the roles played by each function.
- Individuals were challenged to realign their efforts, ensuring focus on agreed-to priorities.
- They ensured consistency of messages within a specific time frame.
- Every leader took on the role of coach. Leaders at all levels of the organization were expected to effectively communicate the strategies to their respective teams and help them translate their actions into their daily roles.
- All employees were able to articulate what actions they were taking to contribute to the successful execution of the tactics that aligned with the respective strategies.
- All employees had a renewed sense of purpose, understanding how and where they could contribute to business success. As a result of their participation in the ACTION workshops, employees understood the priorities from the perspective of their individual departments.

The Flow of Call to ACTION Workshops

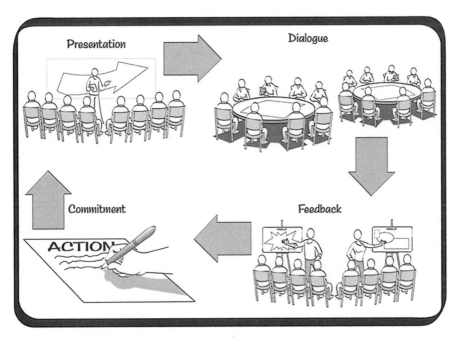

Jim Johnston, a president at the Dr Pepper Snapple Group, said of his experience: "People will get engaged in execution to the level that they believe their efforts contribute to a successful outcome for the business."

Practical Application
Demystifying the Agenda

The Power of Visuals

Could you improve alignment to your business priorities by:

1. Using visuals to translate your business strategy?
2. Demystifying some of the complexities you face?
3. Using visuals to direct efforts against a handful of priorities?
4. Using visual icons to reinforce and maintain momentum against priorities?
5. Using visuals to simplify communications?

The Power of Cross-Functional Workshops

Could you use employee workshops to:

1. Create strong cross-functional collaboration?
2. Translate desired behaviors into practical application?
3. Demystify strategies or change initiatives?
4. Strengthen understanding at all levels?
5. Build greater commitment to and accountability for results?
6. Accelerate your change agenda?

CHALLENGE THREE

All hands on deck

Build capabilities, structure,
and decision authority

Barriers to the Enabling of Effective Change

So far, we have spoken about creating an enthusiasm for the road ahead and an excitement about being a part of the journey—how to get the hearts of your people *engaged*. We then discussed how to bring everyone's head *aligned* behind the highest value-creating priorities, shape new behaviors, and address the misdirected enthusiasm that can create unwanted inertia in your change agenda. Now it is time to effectively *enable* each individual and the team as a whole to deliver to your expected standards.

The first step in enabling effective change is to identify and address the barriers to performance that are implanted in your specific business culture and processes. In general, I have found the following six barriers to be the most counterproductive:

1. Enthusiastic Incompetence

In chapter 4 we discussed "misdirected enthusiasm"—the problematic situation where highly enthusiastic employees invest valuable energies and resources against the wrong priorities. We spent some time discussing how crystal-clear alignment can redirect these energies toward the correct set of goals.

Equally destructive in change initiatives is what I call *enthusiastic incompetence*—a common barrier where enthusiastic and aligned employees flounder because they either lack the necessary knowledge, skills, tools, or decision authority to execute toward the change proposals or are in some way inhibited within the organization's architecture.

I imagine that most of you have experienced frustration after dialing a 1-800 number of an organization that has outsourced its customer service center in order to save costs. Enthusiastically, any question that you asked was answered as long as it was within the pre-determined, scripted answers provided. If you asked any question beyond the script, you no doubt came face-to-face with "enthusiastic incompetence." The unfortunate service provider remained enthusiastic and friendly but was ill equipped to competently address your problem.

Although the operators on the other end of the line usually bear the brunt of our frustrations, their incompetence rests squarely on the shoulders of their leaders, who have failed to enable their employees to succeed in this new, outsourced business model.

Early in my career, I worked for an organization that implemented a change program focusing on building an authentic enthusiasm for customer service in all business processes. In one of our factories, a production manager was very proud of his team's achievements in customer service: 100 percent on-time and in-full deliveries. However, we eventually discovered that the warehouse was carrying significantly higher stock inventories, which adversely impacted working capital and increased product write offs. Why did this happen? The supervisor determined that if we were to fulfill every request from our customers, "just-in-case" inventory was far more important than "just-in-time." His enthusiasm to delight the customers was commendable, but the execution lacked broader business competence.

2. Culture as Your Achilles Heel

Often, when well-established businesses are acquired by private equity, shareholder value doubles or even triples within just a few years.

It's a situation worth exploring: Does private equity possess some magical leadership capabilities, or did the management team of the acquired company lack the competence to unlock this potential?

I believe that within every corporation there lies significant untapped value that is trapped by entrenched mind-sets, practices, and processes that have solidified as norms within the corporate culture. Private equity firms, driven by very clear goals, are able to drive out waste and redundancies by shattering these preconceptions and entrenched practices and, therefore, unlock significant value.

These cultural norms are deeply rooted—sometimes shaped over many years. No doubt that at their inception, these practices had specific and often strategic purposes. In many cases, the rationale for their introduction was sound at the time, and they were initiated to capture a particular opportunity or address a current problem. Unfortunately, the logic and value of these practices, processes, and norms erode in a dynamic business environment but are perpetuated despite outliving their usefulness. The impact of entrenched norms on business performance is significant, and changing these behaviors and mind-sets is often the hardest change a business must undertake. Consider this example:

In May 1996, having spent my first week in a new role as director of organization development for Cadbury Schweppes in London, I was pleasantly surprised to receive an invitation to have dinner with the chairman of the company. I imagined this dinner would be to welcome expatriates, like me, who had recently taken on a post at the London head office.

I was surprised, however, to find out that this invitation was for me alone and that this would be a one-on-one event with the chairman. I was impressed. During dinner, the chairman took

time to explain the set of leadership practices that he strongly believed in—practices that he felt were an important part of the Cadbury Schweppes culture. Now, while his message was delivered in wonderful British subtleties and innuendos, I was left with no uncertainty as to how strongly he wanted these practices retained and that, in my new role, my future endeavors in organizational development were in no way to erode these practices. "In Cadbury Schweppes," he said, "we do not embrace one style of leadership. We offer a myriad of approaches and techniques and allow our business leaders across the world to develop their own unique approaches as long as they operate within the values of the company."

Honestly, the eloquence with which the message was conveyed, enhanced, of course, by excellent cuisine and red wine, left me in awe of what appeared to be a truly sage approach to leadership—an approach which I am sure was birthed out of sound logic and a belief that it would create some competitive advantage. The long-term outcome, however, was less than impressive. Business units across the Cadbury Schweppes world operated as fiefdoms, creating enormous redundancy and duplication of effort. Successful business practices were not shared across the company, and each business developed its unique growth plans. In the 1990s, an evaluation of manufacturing efficiencies revealed an asset utilization of less than 30 percent. Each business was developing unique manufacturing capabilities to expand into and through each other's territories with little if any synergy being realized between the businesses. Brand proliferation and multiple formulations of the same product prevailed, eroding profitability and thus the company's ability to compete effectively and efficiently against international competitors.

Recognizing the urgent need for change, attempts were made to streamline processes and share resources wherever possible. Faced with significant resistance to change, the results were mediocre at best. Business leaders had come to treasure their independence from corporate dictates, and, with the norms of independence firmly embedded, their businesses evolved into impenetrable fiefdoms.

About a year later, all of this would change. John Sunderland was appointed as chief executive officer and, although he was a thirty-year veteran at the time of this appointment, he was willing to challenge the entrenched norms and set about driving fundamental change.

He was very vocal about the fact that for the previous ten years the company had failed to meet the expectations of shareholders. This could not persist. Not only did he introduce a fundamentally different set of business processes, namely value-based management, he aggressively drove cultural change.

He defined the expected leadership characteristics, which were quickly and unconditionally embedded into the people-practices of performance management, talent identification, reward systems, and leadership development. The new organization culture demanded greater accountability for results, quicker adaptability to changing market dynamics, and more aggressive competing in the pursuit of business. He made courageous financial commitments to investors, refused to compromise on expected cultural changes, and made the tough people decisions when necessary.

The step change in business performance evidenced over the next fifteen years would not have occurred had some of these "old organizational truths" not been abandoned or significantly modified.

Often, norms are built off past successes that in the dynamic business environment of today may no longer be relevant. Emerging out of the industrial revolution in Europe, for example, Cadbury created a truly people-centric culture. Considering how poorly employees had been treated at the time, this gave the company a distinct competitive advantage. They were able to attract and retain the best talent. Fast forward to the twenty-first century; these entrenched practices are now seen as paternalistic and overprotective of average performance, eroding clear accountability for results.

To prevent these traps and ensure that the culture and norms we are creating do not become an Achilles heel, we must be vigilant at recognizing, evaluating, and challenging the behaviors that become embedded in our business. We need to review these norms in light of our current and future business strategies, challenging their value-contribution to future strategies.

3. Making Good Performance Punishing

Ironically, embedded business practices can sometimes trigger adverse consequences for employees trying to do the right thing. The following example illustrates how the consequences of misalignment can defy logic:

In the mid-1980s, a company for whom I worked was very frugal about all company spending. In the competitive environment in which it operated, they needed to keep expenses under tight control to allow for aggressive pricing while protecting margins. In the drive to cut costs, every department explored ways to minimize unnecessary spending.

One department, transportation, introduced a policy to inspect all company vehicles on an annual basis—not only to be certain that the assets were being well maintained but also to decide if vehicles needed replacement. They determined that company vehicles would only be replaced when mechanics deemed a vehicle to be in such condition that maintenance costs would outweigh the cost of leasing a new vehicle. Management agreed that this seemed like a logical plan.

But for one particular sales representative who loved cars, this policy proved to be punishing. Because he took exceptional care of his company-provided vehicle (weekly washings, cautious driving, timely maintenance), under this new policy, his applications to have his aging car replaced were repeatedly declined. Unlike his peers, whose worn-out vehicles were readily replaced, his car was in immaculate condition, and, as a result, year after year, he experienced the same outcome—the consequence for his care of the company asset was that he got to keep it for another year.

In desperation, he made a poor and irrational decision. He poured sugar into the gas tank of his company car, causing engine seizure. As a consequence, he lost his job for damaging company property.

What led this dedicated, high-performing employee to behave so irrationally? Due to leadership's failure to understand the unintended consequences of a seemingly logical policy, this employee's positive behavior ultimately had become a punishment. The policy failed to align positive consequences with new expected behaviors.

So good performance can be punishing. Business processes and policies, implemented with all the right intentions, can sometimes trigger unintended negative consequences for those trying to operate within them.

4. Rewarding Poor Performance

Equally, bad performance can be rewarded when incentives do not take into account the adverse impact of behaviors employees might take to maximize payouts. Often, these inappropriate behaviors are as a consequence of a narrow business perspective but can at times be deliberate and self-serving. The latter is demonstrated by the following example:

In one of our manufacturing environments, we created an incentive program that rewarded the efficient use of production hours. The measure established was manufacturing man-hours per ton of product produced: a feasible measure with a meaningful incentive, or so we believed. We soon saw incentive payouts increasing and assumed that the incentive was working effectively. However, this was not the case.

Members of one production team quickly realized they could earn their incentive bonus by concentrating on those products where the setup time, cleaning time, and lower-line stoppages translated into a lower man-hours-per-ton measure. As a consequence, less focus was given to the more complex products that required greater setup time within the production process.

The result was excessive inventories of certain products, excessive warehouse utilization, and, ultimately, obsolescence, as well as short supply of other products in the portfolio.

We would like to believe that individuals naturally focus their efforts on important matters and sacrifice personal agendas for a more universal good. However, that's not always the case. As previously noted, individuals tend to invest their time in that which gives them the greatest reward and the least amount of pain. As leaders driving fundamental change, then, we must not only ensure that outcomes associated with the actions and behaviors of our people are clearly aligned with positive and significant rewards; we must also arrange meaningful negative consequences for nonconformance as well.

If there is little differentiation in the rewards and consequences for strong and poor performance, the chances are that performance will gravitate to the average. Consider the annual compensation review process. If the difference between an outstanding performance rating and an average performance rating amounts to a mere 1 or 2 percent merit increase, why do we believe that individuals will exert exceptional effort for so small a differentiator? If we want to drive fundamentally higher standards of performance, we must ensure a significant, meaningful upside linked to that delivery. Equally, we must create negative consequences for nonperformance that will drive the necessary positive behavior change or lead nonperformers to opportunities outside the company both for their benefit and that of the organization.

5. Squeezing the Balloon

Introducing change into any system or environment results in ripple effects that must be anticipated and managed. It is, therefore, critical to proactively and continuously review the entire value chain within which change is being implemented. Think of the impact of squeezing a balloon. Squeezing one area simply causes another part of the balloon to expand. This action does not remove the air from the balloon but merely displaces it. Failing to maintain a holistic view of the entire value chain within which we are introducing change can be synonymous with squeezing a balloon, merely shifting the pressure and demands from one part of the organization to another.

I experienced this phenomenon after an outside consultant recommended that our company outsource most of our HR functions and establish "employee self-serve" as an efficient alternative. The principle was sound—by using a third party and leveraging technology, we could significantly reduce costs by eliminating HR support staff. However, a meaningful portion of the savings introduced in the proposal would in effect have been squeezing one side of the balloon. What the consultant did not address was the adverse impact on managers' time—we needed salespeople maximizing their selling time, and we did not want highly paid leaders spending their valuable time on matters such as updating their benefit plans, entering address changes, querying medical claims, etc.

The opportunity costs associated with these types of changes, though difficult to measure, must be carefully examined and taken into account. Shifting expense and complexity from one part of the value chain to another does not constitute effective change.

6. Not Catching People Doing Things *Right*

As people develop new skills and behaviors, they will make mistakes—the road can be messy and awkward. Leaders with Type A personalities often show intolerance with anything other than perfection from the get-go. While the pursuit of perfection may in general be a good attribute, it becomes disengaging when constant criticism overshadows compliments. We must take time to reward small victories on the road to the ultimate goal rather than gravitate to deficiencies.

Some of you may have experienced a time when your child brought home a school report card that showed results something like this: A, A, A, B+, B+, B-, C. Which of these grades did you tend to consider first? Chances are, if you're a Type A personality, you zoomed right in and challenged the C. I'm not suggesting that we ignore the C, but perhaps we should start with the As and Bs—celebrate the successes, and then we can lead into a coaching approach on how to get from a C to a B- and then to a B and so forth.

The same applies to change within an organization. Seek out opportunities to catch people doing things *right* as they move toward excellence.

Make heroes of those who become champions of the cause. Your people will become energized by what you prioritize and what you reinforce with both positive and negative consequences. Remember, individuals will invest their time in that which gives them the greatest reward and the least amount of pain.

When you catch and celebrate people doing things right, you are out there "where the action is" and looking for opportunities to recognize achievement. You can effectively inspect what you expect, practically and pragmatically monitoring performance. When you are on the front lines at the point of execution, you can identify and immediately address performance obstacles, once again sending the right cues and clues to your people about your commitment to their success.

Practical Application
Barriers to the Enabling of Effective Change

Enthusiastic Incompetence
1. Have you equipped your team to handle the complexities of the change?
2. How positive will the changes appear to your customers?

Culture as Your Achilles Heel
1. How can you embed *constant change* as the new norm?
2. Are you building change-management capabilities at all levels of leadership?
3. Is your team proud of its ability to adapt quickly and decisively to change?
4. Are you recognizing and rewarding those who constructively challenge the status quo?
5. Are you keeping in touch with what's changing in your industry and other industries?

Reward the Right Behaviors
Are there policies and procedures that, if left unchanged, could:
- Trigger ineffective or inappropriate behavior?
- Blur accountability for results?
- Create uncertainty about decision authority?

Squeezing the Balloon
How well have you thought through the ripple effects of this change?
1. What complexity or workload could you be shifting elsewhere in the business?
2. Are the results of your change generating true business-wide benefits?

3. What controls and measures are in place to monitor questions one and two above?

To Catch People Doing Things Right

1. What formal and informal reward systems do you have in place to catch people doing things right?
2. What progress milestones have you set, and how will you celebrate accomplishment?
3. If your change agenda demands cross-functional collaboration, how will you recognize this combined effort?

Building Core Capabilities

Whenever we implement change, whether it's through an acquisition, merger, reorganization, or the introduction of a new business process, we need to identify and build the capabilities necessary for success. Demands for new skill sets and ways of working will emerge as ripple effects of change, and we must be diligent about providing learning opportunities. "If we don't train them," says CEO Larry Young, "we can't blame them."

In today's competitive environment, we must be able to respond quickly to change. We are challenged to develop programs that effectively impart and instill essential knowledge and skills in a manner that is least disruptive to the business, in the shortest time and at the lowest cost. We can no longer afford the luxury of a traditional formal approach to training. We also cannot afford to compromise on critical training standards. Many change initiatives fail for this reason. The newly formed Dr Pepper Snapple Group faced this challenge.

Within nine months of the business integration, disparate businesses with employees spread over more than two hundred locations in three countries had been thrown together at an accelerated pace in order to go public. Across the newly formed organization, there were many views on how best to make, sell, and distribute soft drinks. These entrenched approaches lacked any uniformity and soon resulted in counterproductive activity, creating significant inertia across the newly formed organization.

We needed to develop practical and efficient methods to impart knowledge, set standards, and build the skill sets necessary for success.

Just As Needed, Just Enough, Just in Time, and Just Right

Partnering with ej4, an organization that builds content for online training, we created a portal that became the remote campus for all twenty thousand employees of Dr Pepper Snapple. The ej4 company name ("e" for electronic and "j4" for the four fundamentals introduced by the word "just") encompasses the greatest strength of its approach: providing online training that is "just as needed" (rookies need different content than veterans need); "just enough" (very short videos sequentially arranged to accommodate short attention spans); "just in time" (content provided immediately prior to need); and "just right" (never boring). Every core capability was addressed step-by-step in a timely fashion and in an engaging way. Using this methodology, we addressed the common objections we heard from learners:

"This doesn't apply to me" was addressed by providing content customized to each learner's degree of experience. Rookies got the basics while veterans saw more advanced tactics. Ej4 uses very inexpensive green-screen technology to make creation of custom content affordable. That is just as needed.

"I don't have time" was addressed with very short videos that could be "squeezed in" to the workday. We would say, "What do you mean you don't have time? You certainly can find ten minutes sometime during your day, can't you?" Everyone could be held accountable for ten minutes to learn something new. That is just enough.

"The training comes too late or too early" was addressed by making it available twenty-four hours a day, seven days a week from any web-enabled device anywhere that Internet access was possible. Learners could even watch their training modules from smartphones in their vehicles in a customers' parking lot immediately prior to the moment the capability had to be executed. That is just in time.

"Training is boring" was addressed by encompassing humor, attractive graphics, and tightly scripted content delivered by engaging presenters. We flipped the learning by making "lecture" happen as homework and "coaching" happen one-on-one with our newly trained and empowered coaches. That is just right.

Together, we created a powerful web-hosted tool, entitled the "Dr Pepper Snapple Campus" (DPS Campus). Through this vehicle, we provided employees with focused, efficient, and relevant training essential to the embedding of vital knowledge and skills deep into the organization. This initiative, personally endorsed by Jim Johnston, divisional president at Dr Pepper Snapple, continues to be a huge success:

> The Dr Pepper Snapple Campus has been an incredibly powerful tool, enabling accelerated learning. With our rapid rate of change, we expect our people to operate at higher levels of effectiveness. This calls for accelerated learning and capability development from all our employees in order to compete effectively to win.

A critical step in this process was to equip everyone who managed the performance of one or more employees to become an effective coach and developer of others. We brought this to life by developing and rolling out a series of training videos under the banner of "Leader as Coach."

We also issued a mandate that all of the over three thousand leaders take part in this training on the DPS Campus with the requirement that every leader was to be an effective coach. If we expect our employees to achieve superior performance, then we, as leaders, must provide them with the necessary training.

With the integration of our businesses, we had experienced conflicting standards of performance. This dissonance was not the consequence of malicious intent. On the contrary, we had individuals doing their absolute best to support the initiative the only way they knew how—by incorporating the methods that they had already used with success. The problem had resided squarely in their differing expectations and guidelines. With our new coaching capabilities, we were able to develop practical methods to embed new processes, help set new standards, and measure performance. Coaches, now trained on *how* coaching was expected to be done, were equipped with the *what* of the coaching process.

Through the DPS Campus, leaders had access to teaching notes, short videos, workbooks, guides, templates, and training modules. They coached their own teams, lending value and credibility to the learning process. Additionally, this coordinated, company-wide training effort enabled the Dr Pepper Snapple Group to achieve consistency across the organization.

I believe that employees gain more value from a less-than-eloquent presentation by their manager who understands their roles and can impact their careers than from a dynamic delivery by a consultant or someone from the corporate office.

To enable leaders to effectively use the material on the DPS Campus, programs were supported with leader notes, templates, and lesson plans.

In a short time, individuals who had lacked confidence in training and public speaking were exhibiting markedly increased abilities. Across the organization, line-manager coaching embedded common standards and processes and created healthy momentum in business performance. When we equip managers to become effective coaches, we serve another valuable purpose—coaching sessions enabled powerful two-way dialogue. Leaders tapped into their teams' ideas and experiences when translating the new DPS practices into their day-to-day activities.

"Leader as Coach" is one of the most powerful principles we introduced into the company. It holds leaders accountable to impart knowledge and skills to their people, as well as to provide ongoing feedback on performance against identified business priorities. They serve as mentors, striving to help their people to succeed. This continuous focus on the handful of priorities forces leaders to coach their people on what to start doing, what to continue doing, and what to stop doing—the latter often the most difficult of the three. As Rodger Collins, president of packaged beverages with Dr Pepper Snapple Group, testifies:

> Having identified and clearly communicated the priorities for the business has enabled me, as an executive, to move away from the cascading of objectives to my people, and instead directly involve them in translating these priorities into business opportunities that they themselves identify and put forward to me. This creates a real ownership and determination to succeed against the objectives that they have identified and set. This has transformed performance management from being an arbitrary HR process.

Another feature of the DPS Campus was the unique login ID assigned to every employee. This strategy allowed us to monitor and ensure individual participation. The campus soon became a powerful enabler on four fronts:

1. Rolling Out Messages from the Top

Through five- to ten-minute videos, the CEO or any other senior executive could expeditiously cascade key messages to the entire organization. With the speed at which the business dynamics were changing, the Campus became an essential tool to keep employees informed and engaged.

With DPS Campus monitoring, we ensured that everyone received the messages, and, by empowering leaders to be coaches of their own staff, we ensured that key messages were not lost in translation. Dilution of message is often a major problem in the cascading of communications from leadership.

2. Aligning Cross-Functional Efforts

Using the DPS Campus, we were able to align cross-functional efforts by efficiently and effectively cascading:

- Sales, marketing, and operations information.
- Strategies pertaining to new brand launches.
- Major sales promotions, including positioning, pricing, listings, availability, and specifications.

The online videos enhanced sales meetings and ensured a united front in the execution of key business initiatives.

3. Compliance to New Standards

As a newly formed organization, we were understandably troubled by, among other areas of concern, a lack of compliance in people practices, safety standards, and expense management. Using the DPS Campus, we rolled out new standards, ensuring compliance in multiple business processes. By monitoring activity and completion, we were able to ensure 100 percent awareness of newly introduced compliance policies and standards.

4. Imparting Knowledge and Skills

The DPS campus became widely used for the building of core DPS capabilities in a number of disciplines. From managing people performance, inventory control, revenue and margin management, and selling skills, the DPS campus became the vehicle of choice for the building of these capabilities.

As we put various businesses together, we were faced with a tremendous opportunity to sell a much wider portfolio of leading brands across the entire United States. But many of our seasoned salespersons had little if any exposure to, much less experience with, selling so many of the brands within our post-integration portfolio. The DPS Campus became a powerful tool in building the necessary sales and trade knowledge of the brands in an effective manner.

5. Equipping Leaders as Coaches

Expecting leaders to step up and become coaches should not assume that there are uniformity and acceptable standards in the knowledge, skills, and behaviors of all people in leadership. The DPS Campus, therefore, served as a powerful tool to guide the content and standards for all leaders when embarking upon their roles as coaches. Critical content for the new business processes was conveyed through the Campus first to leaders and then, through their coaching efforts, made available throughout the organization.

Practical Application
Building Core Capabilities

As you drive your change agenda, consider the knowledge and skills (capabilities) needed for your initiative to succeed:

1. How clearly have you defined these new capabilities?
2. What is the most effective way to build these capabilities?
3. Can you equip leaders at every level to be coaches of the new?
4. If so, how will you equip them and hold them accountable?
5. How can you effectively communicate and embed changes in expectations and capabilities as they arise along the journey?
6. With the dynamics of change, how efficiently and effectively can you get key messages to all employees to retain engagement, alignment, and enablement?

Understanding the Learning Journey

As we implement change and help our people adapt to the new, how aggressively should we drive the initiative and become intolerant of nonconformance? I have participated in many change agendas, and this question has triggered heated debates. There is clearly an argument to support swift and aggressive change implementation to signal urgency and, in some cases, seize first-mover advantage. However, the quality of implementation can be sorely compromised if the learning curve needed for the new skill, tool, or process is not understood or anticipated. How long is long enough will depend on a number of factors that contribute simultaneously to the potential outcome:

- The complexity of the new skills or processes—how realistic is your time frame to allow individuals to acquire the new skills and operate to standard using the new processes?
- The training, coaching, and support—to what extent will you provide assistance to accelerate the learning curve?
- The consequences associated with change—how meaningful are the consequences associated with change agenda?
- The deadlines and milestones for implementation—how will you clarify and communicate the target dates for completion?

Coaching through Change

When I lead discussions on the critical components of change, I refer to a simple model that I call the "ESP of Coaching through Change."

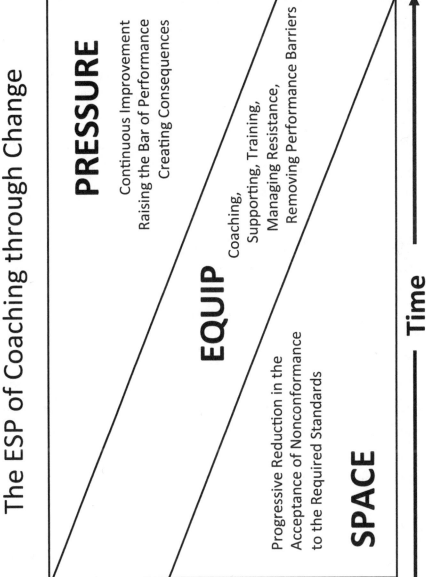

The ESP of Coaching through Change

PRESSURE
Continuous Improvement
Raising the Bar of Performance
Creating Consequences

EQUIP
Coaching,
Supporting, Training,
Managing Resistance,
Removing Performance Barriers

SPACE
Progressive Reduction in the
Acceptance of Nonconformance
to the Required Standards

Time

In the above diagram, the time frame is dependent on the complexity of the new skill or behavior being coached. The more complex or demanding the change, the longer the adoption time will be. As leader, your role is to determine what the time for full adoption of the new should be and to effectively apply the E, S, and P of coaching:

Equip refers to the guidance, training, feedback, and support that will be provided to the team—or individual—in order to meet the new standards within the specified time frame. This preparation is ongoing throughout the learning journey. Learners must be clear about the training you will be providing, what the expected standards of new performance are, when they need to meet these standards, and how you will determine if they have met them. There should be no surprises. The consequences of failing to achieve expected standards must be unambiguous and consistently applied.

Space refers to the leeway you will give as people work through the learning curve. How much wiggle room or below-standard delivery will you allow along the journey from the current to the new? As the visual illustrates, supported by regular feedback, this latitude needs to be reduced progressively as we move toward the deadline by which standards are to be met. Be sure to clarify expected standards of improvement at various stages along the learning journey and address obstacles to performance that might arise.

Pressure refers to the amount of positive coercion you will apply to consistently raise performance standards within expected time frames, and to ensure that the consequences associated with noncompliance are understood. Implicit in this action is also the understanding that those who meet and retain new standards will be publicly recognized.

This simple ESP diagram can be useful in the facilitation of discussions with management—helping them recognize the need for their personal involvement in the coaching process and their need to demonstrate consistency in expectations and consequences.

At the end of the designated—and clearly communicated—time period, some individuals may fail to meet the new standards, but this should come as no surprise to them or to you. You will have walked with them through the change journey, given them the necessary coaching and support, constructively increased the pressure to conform to expectations by reducing the wiggle room, and clearly explained the consequences associated with failing to meet standards.

Practical Application
Understanding the Learning Journey

Changing behaviors and applying new skills is never an easy undertaking. As leader, consider the ESP of change and ask these questions:

1. How comprehensive is the training you will be providing?
2. Will the training be true skills development or education?
3. How will you evaluate whether standards have been met?
4. Have the consequences for nonperformance been made *very* clear ("no-surprises management")?
5. How will regular, constructive feedback be provided, and by whom?
6. Are performance standards at various intervals of change well understood?
7. To reduce wiggle room, what potential obstacles to performance must be removed?
8. What positive pressure will you apply to consistently raise performance standards?
9. How will you publicly recognize those who meet and retain new standards?
10. How will you ensure consistency in your management of performance?
11. What tough people decisions are you prepared to make?

Enabling "Real"
Work to Happen

D espite corporate's best strategies and marketing investments, brand equity is ultimately built or eroded after customers become familiar with a product or service. Every day, frontline employees deliver critical "moments of truth" that shape customer loyalty.

Think of your own positive or negative experiences at the check-in counter at an airport, for example, or while shopping in a department store.

No marketing effort can sufficiently offset the impact of a negative encounter with a disinterested service provider—this kind of experience can indelibly shape a customer's view of the product. Likewise, intrinsic value intensifies after a significant positive experience.

In the hectic agendas associated with major organizational change, the priorities of meeting short-term goals often outweigh the critical dimension of enabling frontline employees. A fundamental success factor in implementing change is our ability to translate new strategies into practical tactics that can be executed daily by those who are selling, making, and distributing products and services to customers. Through a deliberate process of strategy translation, we can build relevance and delegate the necessary authority to enable customer-centered actions at every level in the organization.

How can we tap into the wealth of knowledge and experience that our valuable frontline operators possess? Many of these people are employees whose jobs often confine them to the execution of repetitive and transactional activities—we seldom engage them in broader business challenges, nor do they expect to be engaged. There is much evidence to show, however, that companies that engage, align, and enable the efforts of all employees, regardless of their positions in the hierarchy, leverage the full power of their human capital.

The ACTION Huddle

In chapter 6, I described the Dr Pepper Snapple's Call to ACTION workshops that focused on their seven thousand salaried employees. The following is a description of the novel process that was designed and implemented to enable the rest of the team—the frontline employees—to participate in strategy execution.

Dr Pepper Snapple recognized how essential the aligned efforts of its more than thirteen thousand employees who hold critical operational frontline positions were to its success. To build their business understanding and enable these employees to contribute to strategy within their areas of accountability, the company implemented what we called "Call to ACTION Huddle Sessions."

These one- to two-hour workshops generated practical ideas on how to improve processes, drive out waste, and increase quality. By creating these forums, we enabled people to contribute to business priorities by translating the key strategies into their areas of decision authority. Rather than spend significant sums of money on consultants or engineers to do workflow studies and process improvements, we were able to tap into the vast experience of our employees, whose knowledge and talents were often overlooked. Who better to identify areas for process improvement and waste reduction than a team of dedicated employees who have been working together for years?

We created an environment and facilitated processes that encouraged their potential. As a result of the time spent with our frontline employees on process improvement, we were able to recognize and remove the management-created obstacles that hindered improvement. These obstacles resulted from policies and procedures that, though well intended, were developed without input from those who must live with the consequences of added bureaucracy. They were hindering cogs in the machinery of business processes—they eroded effectiveness and efficiencies.

By repositioning the importance of frontline roles, we were able to bring about a fundamental change in attitudes between frontline employees and those in leadership positions. This shift created an environment in which the input of seasoned operators was valued, recognized, and acted upon.

The ACTION Huddle Sessions allowed us to translate our business challenges and opportunities into the everyday realities of our frontline employees. As a result, they were able to leverage their vast experience and identify opportunities for improvement.

Once again, we used visuals to present the goals of our initiative. The following is one of many examples that helped build context and relevance, which illustrates the impact of individual actions on overall performance.

With more than nine thousand Dr Pepper Snapple delivery vehicles on the road daily, truck wheel and tire damage occurs regularly and generates a cost of approximately three hundred dollars per wheel and tire to repair or replace. In the soft drink business, the average bottom-line profit on a case of twenty-four cans of soda amounts to about one dollar. To offset the expense of one damaged truck tire and rim, we needed to sell more than three hundred additional cases of product. When we translated that expense into incremental sales needed to offset this expense, our employees were able to understand the impact of their day-to-day activities on overall company performance.

Impact of Day-to-Day Actions on Strategy

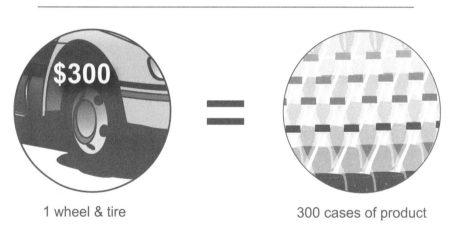

1 wheel & tire   300 cases of product

Visual illustrations were powerful tools to help us translate a number of business realities to our teams. Many realized, perhaps for the first time, that, with small profit margins, saving a penny per case does add up. The mantra of "finding a penny per case" became ingrained into the Huddle sessions. Teams soon identified opportunities to streamline processes and improve operating procedures. The results were truly amazing.

As you plan your change programs, then, consider the dormant untapped knowledge, skills, and experience within your employee base. What practical steps can you take to truly elicit and value this resource? Be creative. Think of novel and practical ways to enable your people to contribute with the confidence that their ideas will be heard and valued.

The following is a simple, innovative idea that encouraged employees to participate in the growth of their company:

Quality Carte Blanche

Several years ago, the beverage division of Cadbury Schweppes South Africa embarked upon a quality improvement program that embraced the principles and practices espoused by Dr. W. Edwards Deming. The program was tracking well—employees were already engaged, aligned, and enabled behind the agenda.

As a part of the program, we introduced a simple but practical tool that enabled all employees to participate in our relentless pursuit of quality. Every individual was issued a "credit card"—with a difference. We called this our "Quality Carte Blanche," which gave the holder the authority, regardless of position, to speak up on issues hindering our pursuit of excellence. On the back of the card, signed by our CEO, was the following declaration:

"This card empowers the holder

to challenge nonconformance to
quality anywhere in the business,
without fear of retribution."

We experienced numerous examples of individuals, Carte
Blanche Card in hand, approaching their managers to constructively
challenge existing methods, often suggesting improvements to
those processes. Others wrote out their ideas or concerns, attaching
photocopies of their Carte Blanche Card. People were enabled to
act and to think outside the norm. Who better to improve business
processes than those who implement them daily? Consider this
example:

**Our company had always embraced an open door policy, but
it was unusual for an employee—in this case, a production line
operator—to interrupt an executive meeting.**

Clasping his Carte Blanche in both hands, the machine operator sought out the production executive. With a shaky voice, he said, "We've stopped production. We have a problem that needs your immediate attention."

The head of production shot to his feet and left the boardroom with the troubled operator. We all wondered what magnitude of crisis had erupted to warrant such a bold act.

A short time later, when the head of production returned, he responded to the CEO's query that he "resolved the problem, which wasn't a big problem after all." But the CEO wanted more details.

"Well, a twenty-thousand-gallon batch of soda concentrate has been mixed with a different ingredient from what the recipe calls for. However," he stated with a sense of accomplishment, "I personally checked with Marketing and Research & Development. They tested the product, and there is no difference in taste or shelf life, and there are no legal implications as a consequence of this ingredient being substituted. My recommendation is that we should go ahead and bottle the product for distribution."

The CEO recognized that for the Quality Improvement Program we were implementing throughout the organization, this was a defining moment—a moment of truth. The definition of quality we had been espousing was nonnegotiable. It was based on Deming's definition: "conformance to predetermined standards." The CEO asked if this batch of concentrate—with the different ingredient—conformed to our predetermined standards.

The operations director recognized the organizational significance of leading by example and conceded that the batch did deviate from this product's predetermined standards: "We'll dump the batch and start again."

The factory followed the order and discarded the entire batch at a significant cost to the company. Although that act to some people might seem wasteful, this was an investment that truly reinforced our unwavering commitment to quality. The decision spread like wildfire through the organization's grapevine.

The message was clear: (1) management was serious about the quality initiative, and (2) feedback about quality issues or opportunities would be embraced. This one production line operator initiated a chain reaction of quality-centered activities that helped instill a commitment to quality across the business.

Though we had incurred a production loss, our quality initiative gained newfound momentum. Had the CEO not adhered to the quality guideline, that news would have just as quickly cascaded throughout the organization, likely undermining the entire quality initiative.

Put yourself in the shoes of this operator. Why did he believe that his actions would not have negative repercussions? He courageously stepped forward, trusting that management would honor his actions. Through consistency of both messaging and actions by leadership, we were able to create an environment that built the required level of trust and respect for the contributions of all employed.

Practical Application
Enabling "Real" Work to Happen

Successful change calls for more than merely engaging frontline employees. It requires that you, as leader, enable them as well by cultivating the wealth of knowledge and experience that they can bring to the organization.

Think about the following:

1. How ready and able is your leadership team to tap into the wealth of knowledge and experience of your frontline employees? How can you leverage/change that?
2. What vehicles/forums/techniques can you use to unlock the potential of your frontline employees to contribute to your initiative?
3. What practical examples (e.g., truck wheel and tire damage costs) could you use to increase pragmatism of your change agenda?
4. How could you practically translate your high-level goals into the day-to-day activities of all your people?

Pass the baton

SUSTAIN

Fuel employee-led
change momentum

Building Unstoppable Momentum

At this stage of our change initiative, we're making great progress. We have *engaged* the hearts of our people behind the vision; we've *aligned* their efforts behind the most important priorities, and their heads are in the game; and furthermore, we have *enabled* superior performance by removing organizational barriers and building core competencies and behaviors.

There remains, however, one more challenge.

You have created a deep-rooted bias for action that you must now sustain. Without *you* continually beating the drum to keep the agenda top of mind, how can you prevent the seemingly inevitable erosion of the initiative? The challenge is knowing how to embed employee-led continuous improvement deep within your organization. To do this, you must focus on the building of "resonance" and maintaining "relevance."

Firstly, let me discuss the concept of resonance. In physics, resonance occurs when a system is able to store and easily transfer energy. At certain resonance frequencies, even small, periodic driving forces can produce large-amplitude oscillations because the system stores vibrational energy.

How does this apply to your change initiative? Having created tremendous energy behind your agenda, your role is to ensure its continued transfer—building the resonance that sustains the momentum of change. When you build resonance into your change agenda, it requires no more than leadership's continued support and encouragement to create unstoppable momentum within an empowered team.

The second requirement for true sustainability is ensuring that this newly created resonance is complemented with *relevance*. As leader, it is your responsibility to ensure that the change agenda is kept fresh and relevant and that the culture of continuous improvement is passed on and continues to grow from one generation of leaders to the next.

Sustainability, then, is the ability to achieve resonance and ensure continued relevance of the change agenda you are leading.

To create *resonance,* we must:

1. Implement waves of change as extensions of the current change agenda.
2. Embed processes and disciplines that facilitate continuous-improvement efforts.
3. Give the ownership of progress monitoring and reporting to employees.
4. Embed new processes and disciplines to avoid regression.

To maintain *relevance,* we must:

1. Move continuous improvement from an interruptive model to an integrated model.
2. Continually revise incentives and structures.
3. Build change leaders for the future.

We will explore these requirements for sustainability in detail.

Creating Resonance

1. Implement waves of change as extensions of the current change agenda.

At this point, your employees have embarked upon the change journey you are calling for, and you have directed their efforts behind a set of priorities and behaviors that they now believe in. But change is a continuous journey and not an end result. At times, you may need to adapt priorities and focus in response to shifting market dynamics, competitive threats, and economic factors.

Furthermore, as change normally requires pioneering into previously uncharted waters, we learn by doing, and we often need to alter course while the project is in flight.

Your challenge is to manage these shifts in a manner that neither confuses people nor erodes your credibility as a leader. Employees must understand the link between the current and the new—what you have them *currently* rallied behind and the new areas that now require attention. This context building is critical.

When employees see the relevance of each wave of change and how it builds on the outcomes of their previous change efforts (time, focus, and energies), the momentum of change will accelerate. If, on the other hand, the change is not seen as an extension of their work, the new priorities will be discounted. We must clearly demonstrate how each wave of change builds upon the constructive work they have already achieved and how it takes the organization and the team to new heights of competitive advantage.

In the event your change agenda must be modified, refer back to The Engagement Cycle guidelines (chapter 1) as you plan the communication of the changes you wish to introduce. If done well, you can both maintain change momentum and at the same time have your people take accountability for its continuous improvement.

In 2011, Dr Pepper Snapple introduced enhancements to their Call to ACTION program. When it was first developed in 2008, the objective of the Call to ACTION initiative was to increase gross sales and crush costs. Five strategic priorities and six ACTION behaviors had been identified and presented to twenty thousand employees. The new project did not alter the original program; rather, it strengthened it—building tremendous sustainability into the fabric of the organization and changing the focus from a "Call to ACTION" to "Team DPS in ACTION." The ACTION behaviors were refreshed to support higher levels of performance and continuous improvement, but the essence of the ACTION behaviors remained unchanged. Thus the initiative sustained continuity while embracing new challenges. This continuity of messaging, alignment of efforts, and recognition of great progress has helped the team seamlessly transition from one wave of change to the next.

2. Embed processes and disciplines that facilitate continuous-improvement efforts.

As we drive for higher standards of performance and efficiency, we empower our people when we embed processes and disciplines and effectively assign decision authority.

If we empower people to drive change but fail to provide the necessary tools and support, employee commitment can lead to misdirected enthusiasm or enthusiastic incompetence.

When this happens, management will be challenged to redirect wrong, albeit well-intended, efforts without demoralizing team members.

There are a number of effective tools and disciplines available to build and sustain a continuous change agenda. I have seen Deming's quality circles, or Tom Peters' *In Search of Excellence*, for example, used with great success. However, I have also seen failures where the introduction of such tools lacked alignment and context with business priorities. Seen as yet another management idea, their introduction failed to gain the traction necessary to drive meaningful change.

Regardless of the tools you use, the critical component for creating and maintaining success with continuous improvement is empowering all employees to take ownership and drive positive changes in their daily activities. This can be accomplished when you provide them with the necessary processes, training, coaching, and support and when you utilize their years of experience to build powerful cross-functional collaboration.

Learning by Doing

Avoid the trap of an extensive ramp-up training period prior to the implementation of change-management tools and processes. Getting everyone trained first might sound good in theory, but, in my experience, this is an expensive route, and executives bore easily! You need to deliver meaningful results *quickly* and, thereafter having gained credibility with leadership and employees, present a holistic plan as to how you will embed this continuous improvement into the entire operation or organization.

I have found the following approach to be successful in gaining support and momentum:

- Identify a significant business process, one that, if improved, would meaningfully impact business performance.
- Get commitment to evaluate the process to identify opportunities for improvement.
- Set an improvement goal that leaders agree is stretching, meaningful, and quantifiable.
- Secure a seasoned facilitator, one who has experience with the change tools you plan to introduce. This facilitator could be someone from within the company or an external consultant.
- Carefully select the senior leaders and influencers you want to involve in the process.
- Have this group and key operators within the identified business process participate actively in a facilitated session in which your chosen tools for continuous improvement are applied to the specific business process.
- Ensure that the identified changes are implemented and that their benefits are quantified.

- Use this and other successes as substantive evidence in building support for your department-wide or company-wide continuous-improvement initiative.

Lay a Foundation of Continuous-Improvement Disciplines and Behavior

Having generated meaningful results through your focus on a few core processes, it's time to now embed the disciplines of continuous improvement within the entire team. Ensure that the tools and processes you select are both practical and can be effectively transferred to your employees to facilitate. You want to systematically, and as quickly as possible, reduce dependency on both external and internal experts, having your own team both facilitating and owning the processes.

This builds your team's confidence in its ability to drive continuous improvement and begins to lay the important foundation of collaborative continuous improvement.

The systematic layering of new concepts, processes, skills, and behaviors embeds continuous improvement into the fiber of your organization. It becomes "the way we do things around here." In Dr Pepper Snapple, the vehicle used to drive the next major wave of change was the introduction of rapid continuous improvement (RCI). Using the principles of lean management, a number of practical tools and processes were systematically introduced. "The very best change comes from our people," says Marty Ellen, CFO of Dr Pepper Snapple and a key driver of continuous improvement.

5S

To engage employees at every level and in every operation, the company introduced a simple yet powerful methodology or workplace organization called 5S. The 5S methodology was developed in Japan and follows five rigorous phases of workplace organization. The five Japanese words, translated into English, are: sort, set in order, shine, standardize, and sustain—thus 5S.

Some of you may know what it's like to build something in your garage when the area is a mess—you can't find your tools, and there's no room to move; or try cooking in a cluttered, disorganized kitchen. Similarly, in a work environment where you need to drive continuous improvement, it is essential to first get the workplace organized and prepared for future and ongoing changes.

The process is not complicated, and its introduction soon builds a healthy discipline and pride in having a well-organized work environment. Whether a corporate office, warehouse, or manufacturing plant, this discipline quickly exposes wasted time and resources, allowing employees to develop and be recognized for improvements that positively impact safety, quality, productivity, and costs.

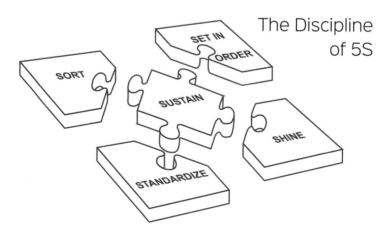

The Discipline of 5S

Dr Pepper Snapple was no exception. 5S gave all employees an opportunity to become involved in improving their work environments and experiencing early wins in continuous improvement.

Business Process Mapping

Building on the 5S mind-set, the team progressively built more impactful continuous-improvement tools and capabilities. As previously discussed, the most successful change initiatives uncover and leverage cross-functional interdependencies. Through collaborative techniques, such as Business Process Mapping, we can break through functional boundaries by collectively reviewing and constructively challenging the value created by every activity within a business process. After all, who knows the intricacies of a business process better than those who operate within it on a daily basis? Using this powerful, cross-functional collaborative process, a team develops a pictorial representation of the flow of all activities within a specific business activity. The transparency of this process enables the team to identify waste in the process and generate solutions that increase efficiency and effectiveness without compromising quality or safety.

Business Process
Mapping

Furthermore, the fact that the team, rather than leadership, has redesigned the process results in an increased ownership of the solution and an accountability to implement the changes that they have identified through collaborative dialogue.

Build Problem-Solving Capabilities Deep into the Organization

Continuous-improvement goals positively challenge employees to achieve new levels of performance, but what happens when, despite their best efforts, they fail to improve a performance metric week after week, month after month?

This scenario can become demoralizing, and it is tempting for the leader to intervene. However, what you want to avoid is a situation where employees, unable to find a solution to a problem, pass it on to management to resolve. To avoid this, we must therefore equip our people with practical techniques to solve problems encountered in their pursuit of continuous improvement. They need the skills and the processes required to analyze problems, find root causes of issues, and generate efficient, effective, and creative solutions to these challenges. These capabilities need to be embedded deep within the organization.

In Dr Pepper Snapple, the team developed a simple and effective process called CAP, or the "Corrective Action Process."

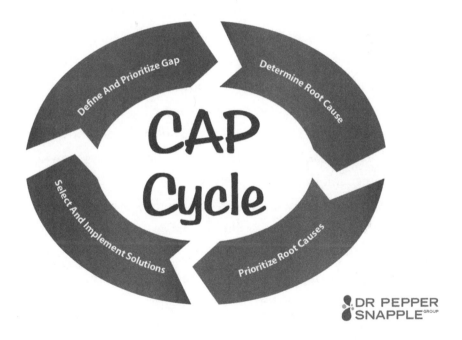

Employees across the organization were trained to use this disciplined process to define performance gaps, uncover and prioritize root causes of problems, and to build, implement, and monitor corrective actions.

The accountability for taking corrective action remained, therefore, with the employees, while leadership provided support and coaching as and when required. The solutions developed by the employees gave them the ownership and the accountability to implement and monitor the impact of their developed solutions.

3. Give the ownership of progress monitoring and reporting to employees.

What's measured gets managed, and when that measurement is open for all to see and monitored by those who perform the tasks, it creates a sustainable degree of accountability. Having translated your change agenda into the activities of every team member, work with them to set up scoreboards that visually represent performance against the stretching goals formerly established. Employees, not management, should own these scoreboards.

Allow every team to display and maintain its results. The visual displays enable teams to discuss progress and challenges and serve as powerful vehicles for leaders to engage with employees by providing coaching, recognition, and support.

It is essential that these displays are designed in such a way that, at a glance, all parties can easily understand performance levels. When well constructed, this visual management of performance improves the quality of dialogue between the leader and the team. The development of an agreed-to layout for scoreboards builds uniformity that enables healthy cross-functional dialogue on performance and opportunities for improvement.

The information on the scoreboards must be data driven, monitoring the most important activities in the improvement process. Additionally, develop and report on leading indicators of performance, namely, those measures that indicate the progress on key drivers that will contribute to the end goal. For example, the number of new sales leads secured serves as a lead indicator of increased future sales. Monitoring lead indicators also enables timely preemptive action when performance indicators are lagging and helps the team determine if it has identified the right drivers of performance.

4. Embed new processes and disciplines to avoid regression.

After processes have been redesigned, we can easily forget to institutionalize the new.

An essential component of change sustainability is the often-neglected discipline of formalizing and embedding redesigned and streamlined processes. Make sure that new procedures are documented, communicated, and built into future training programs.

Ensure that this institutionalizing of newly designed processes becomes core to your business and that you hold teams accountable for the embedding of the new.

If well documented, these newly designed processes, having proven their value in one area of the business, can then be transferred from location to location, function to function, as pragmatic, employee-designed enhancements.

Furthermore, this sharing of new practices creates tremendous opportunities to make heroes of the employees who participated in the process redesign.

Maintaining Relevance

As mentioned earlier, the second requirement for true sustainability is ensuring that the *resonance* created is now complemented with *relevance*.

The change agenda must be kept fresh and relevant, and the culture of continuous improvement must pass on and continue to grow from one generation of leaders to the next.

1. Move continuous improvement from an interruptive model to an integrated model.

When we build continuous-improvement disciplines into the strategy development process, it no longer operates independently as an initiative being undertaken by the business. It is, then, effectively integrated into the way we do business.

Its relevance is sustained when, as part of the annual strategic planning process, a number of key initiatives are flagged for significant improvement. For each of these initiatives, we must plan for "breakthrough change," not "incremental improvements." We must set goals that are truly breakthrough in terms of the challenge they present and the size of the prize when accomplished; we must give accountability for the leadership of these initiatives to our very best talent. It is important to say *no* to pet projects that do not necessarily generate significant business results. These can dilute focus and erode credibility of the change-pioneering culture you want to create.

Ensure that you maintain a holistic assessment and awareness of the company-wide impact of major changes being driven so as to avoid the "squeezing of the balloon" effect referred to earlier in the book. You want to truly drive out waste, not move work elsewhere in the company. You want to drive growth, but not at the expense of brand strategies or margin. Understand the ripple effects of changes being introduced. The impact of your breakthrough changes must score well against a balanced scorecard of metrics.

In Dr Pepper Snapple, all major changes are evaluated to determine their impact on the following critical business dimensions:

Safety—how will this change impact the safety of our employees?

Quality—how will this change impact the quality standards of products and services to customers?

Delivery—how will this impact our delivery of products and services?

Productivity—how will this reduce waste by improving efficiency and/or effectiveness?

Growth—how will this impact short-, medium-, and longer-term business and brand growth?

New processes must contribute positively to one or more of the above without adversely impacting the others. Cascade these breakthrough goals in such a manner that all functions understand their unique contribution and are committed to the breakthrough actions necessary for success.

2. Continually revise incentives and structures.

To sustain continuous change, incentives and structures must be regularly reviewed and updated to support the new behaviors expected. As initiatives are undertaken each year, consider the ripple effects of the planned changes. In light of these changes, determine whether your current incentive programs will drive the behaviors needed to achieve the newly identified breakthrough goals. It is not unlikely that your current incentives, if left unchanged, could encourage behaviors that are less than ideal for the success of your initiatives.

A Dr Pepper Snapple breakthrough goal called for an important change in incentive program design.

The need to shorten production runs in the factory was critical to reducing inventory and warehouse space while retaining excellent customer service levels. This resulted in an increased number of changeovers on the production lines. This required a major overhaul of the processes for changeovers, and through collaborative problem-solving sessions run by the employees, the results were staggering.

Prior to the increase of changeovers, production teams were measured and incented on the Overall Effectiveness of their Equipment—OEE. This measure was based on production effectiveness over the total available hours in any given production shift and did not "discount" for product changeovers. Therefore, keeping these "disruptive" changeovers to a minimum was an important contributor to high incentive payouts.

Increasing changeovers to increase manufacturing flexibility and reduce inventory became far more important than the number of changeovers. As a result, the performance measure was changed to TME, True Mechanical Efficiencies, which removed changeover times from the performance calculation. A separate metric was then put in place to incentivize teams to reduce changeover times through the application of continuous-improvement techniques.

Structures are designed around embedded business processes. Ensure that as you streamline and change processes, you review the organization structure around these processes to determine their continued relevance. Seek out opportunities to flatten structures, automate steps in the process, and delegate authority to speed up decision making.

One of the biggest challenges with the reviewing of structures is the fear of redundancy and job loss. For this reason, employees can be reluctant or at least hesitant to engage in the streamlining of workflow, as its outcome is less work and, ultimately, fewer jobs. As you review structures, therefore, always "use attrition as your friend." Staff turnover of around 8 to10 percent is healthy for most business- es. Remove from people's mind-sets the assumption that vacated roles can be automatically filled. Every time someone leaves the or- ganization, an opportunity is created to redesign a business process and to offer existing staff the opportunity to take on new challenges.

In this environment, you can make a commitment to employees that no one will lose their jobs as a consequence of process redesign. They do, however, need to embrace the idea of being reskilled to take on new and different roles if the process leads to a redesign or elim- ination of their current roles.

3. Build change leaders of the future.

Finally, to ensure the continued relevance of continuous improve- ment and the embedding thereof into an organizational culture, we must develop the next generation of change leaders. The skills, processes, and behaviors that are embodied in your leadership de- velopment programs will ultimately shape and define the behaviors, norms, and culture of your future organization.

By building continuous-improvement skills and disciplines into your leadership development, you send the clear message to all in the organization that their future growth will depend on their abili- ty to gain and apply these capabilities. Building these future change leaders has little to do with classroom training and a great deal to do with learning by doing.

Assigning upcoming leaders to be champions of identified breakthrough change initiatives is, in my experience, the best way to accelerate skills development through real-life application. In sourcing candidates to participate in this critically important development, go straight to your identified high-potential talent pool. These are the "indispensible few" who are normally seen as too essential in their current roles to take on a different assignment. Do not ask for nominations. Those are likely to be candidates who have spare time on their hands. Continuous-improvement leaders *must* be developed from your highest contributing talent, those whom you have identified as the future leaders of the business. Getting them onto this development path achieves a number of important goals:

- It broadcasts the importance of continuous improvement to the company.
- As these highly talented individuals get promoted, it signals to all the career-growth advantage of embracing continuous improvement.
- It helps you filter out those in the talent pool who may not necessarily have the leadership capacity to drive meaningful change.

As resonance begins to build, individuals within your team will surface as true champions of change and continuous improvement. Seize the opportunity to recognize them, and allow them to lead identified improvement opportunities. Give them the necessary change-management tools and decision authority to drive cross-functional initiatives, and provide them with the necessary coaching and support. Begin to build a pipeline of next-generation change leaders.

The Results of Employee-Driven Continuous Improvement

Through 2014, the sustainability of change created by Dr Pepper Snapple has enabled the delivery of impressive, quantifiable results. By empowering their people to own the change agenda, the team has achieved the following:

- Safety—37 percent reduction in recordable accidents.
- Product Quality—25 percent reduction in consumer complaints.
- Delivery Standards—99.9 percent fill rate.
- Productivity—25 percent reduction in warehouse space.
- Growth—50-basis-points increase in market share in their important single-serve market.

Practical Application
Building Unstoppable Momentum

As you review your change initiative, how will you create unstoppable momentum?

Resonance

1. How can you effectively link upcoming change initiatives with the progress already made on the change journey?
2. To build a continuous-improvement culture, what behaviors and norms will need to change? How will you lead this change?
3. What skills and easy-to-use tools can you make available to enable your team to continuously raise the bar of performance?
4. What's the most effective way to embed these skills and tools at all levels?
5. How will you communicate the use of these tools in the context of your change agenda?
6. What clear lead and lag measures have you identified for the key drivers of your change agenda? How measurable are they?
7. How will you create visual management across all functions and have team members own progress-monitoring and reporting?
8. To avoid the delegation of tough problems back to you, how will you equip your team with problem-solving and solution-generation capabilities?
9. What "right" practices will you transfer across the business to accelerate change?

10. How will you standardize new processes to avoid regression to old practices?

Relevance

1. How will you effectively shift continuous improvement from an interruptive process to a truly integrated business process?
2. How will you give the people you have identified as high potential the opportunity to become change agents?
3. Which members of your team are showing potential to become leaders, champions, and coaches of change? How will you accelerate their development?
4. What change-management and continuous-improvement training will you embed into your leadership development programs?
5. With the change you are introducing, what incentive programs need to be revisited?
6. Do the right people have the decision authority to make change happen? Do you need to change the structure?

Conclusion

The percentage of change initiatives that fail to deliver their planned outcomes is staggering. Why is meaningful and lasting change so difficult to achieve, and why do we have a predisposition to gravitate back to our comfort zones?

I was thinking about this dilemma while on a recent business trip. A few minutes into the flight, I could feel the plane beginning to level off and was waiting for the all-clear signal before firing up my computer.

The captain of the plane came on the loudspeaker with the familiar announcement: "Ladies and gentlemen, we have reached our cruising altitude. It is now safe to move about the cabin."

I thought about this announcement and realized how analogous it is to so many change initiatives. There is an exhilarating takeoff and climb when we launch and implement change. But this excitement soon dissipates when we reach "cruising altitude." The sense of urgency and the push to achieve new heights begins to wane.

As the captain of your change initiative, there are two mind-sets you must avoid at all costs:

1. Believing your current progress is safe from erosion.

All too soon, we revel in our progress, believing that the gains we have achieved from the change agenda thus far are securely "in the bank." When complacency creeps in, we fail to anticipate and respond to the countermeasures of our competitors. These competitors are determined to regain any ground they might have lost as a consequence of our initial surge.

2. Achieving a cruising altitude.

The speed and innovation we face in today's competitive business environment means we must never forget that today's excellence is tomorrow's average. When we sense the slightest leveling off of our change agenda, it's time to remobilize the team and buckle up in preparation for the next ascent.

This mind-set must be instilled into your culture throughout the organization in order to fuel personal accountability for the continual pursuit of the better way. "Good enough" soon becomes the enemy of excellence in any endeavor.

After all the years I have spent translating the change agendas of organizations into the daily activities of their employees, I realize there is no silver bullet, no single solution to managing change. However, I have found the steps and processes covered in this book to be powerful contributors to successful change management. When leading your team through these changes, then, aim to:

- Engage their **hearts** behind your vision, namely the preferred future outcome that you will lead them to.
- Align their **heads** around a handful of priorities that they have translated into their day-to-day roles.
- Enable their **hands** to execute by removing obstacles to performance, providing resources, and building the necessary capabilities.
- Sustain the momentum by passing the baton to your team, reducing their dependency on you to drive continuous change.

Only then will you have a truly mobilized team—one capable of creating a sustainable competitive advantage against your competitors.

My hope is that the experiences and ideas I have shared in this book will help you in leading your teams to deliver sustained high performance—performance that, without your leadership, they would not otherwise attain.

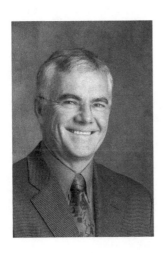

About the Author

Larry Solomon, CEO of Solomon People Solutions, served as executive vice president of human resources for the Dr Pepper Snapple Group (DPS) from 2003 to August 2013. In this role, he was responsible for a company of approximately twenty thousand colleagues in over two hundred facilities across North America and the Caribbean.

As an executive leader, Larry contributed significantly to the company's evolution into an independent, fully integrated beverage business. This includes the consolidation of four separate beverage companies, the acquisition and integration of Dr Pepper/Seven Up Bottling Group and other major independent bottling and distributing businesses, and the establishment of Dr Pepper Snapple (DPS) after the Cadbury Schweppes PLC spinoff in 2008.

Larry's service to DPS and Cadbury has spanned more than twenty-eight years and three continents. He joined the company in 1985 in his native country of South Africa, serving on the board of management as director of human resources for a wholly owned subsidiary. He was then promoted to sales director, leading a large sales force in serving national retail and foodservice accounts for Cadbury Schweppes's beverage business in South Africa before moving internationally with the company. He moved to the United States in 1999 to become senior vice president of human resources for Dr Pepper/Seven Up, Inc. after serving for three years on Cadbury's global HR leadership team in London as director of organizational development

On a personal note, Larry received a training and development diploma through the Institute of Personnel Management in South Africa and an MBA from the University of Texas at Dallas. He and his wife, Charmaine, have four children, Tascha, Tyron, Donovan, and Kyle, and they live in Plano, Texas.